LOW-FAT MEALS IN MINUTES

from the Home Library Test Kitchen

Cole's Home Library Cookbooks
Glen Ellen, California

LOW-FAT MEALS IN MINUTES

Constantly juggling the demands of a busy life with the need to eat a healthy diet can prove difficult, especially when take out so often seems to be the easy option. What you really want are meals that can be on the table in 30 minutes, that adhere to today's nutritional guidelines about eating less fat, but without compromising on flavor. Impossible? Of course not! This fabulous new collection is the answer to a busy cook's prayers – some recipes can be made in minutes, others can be prepared ahead, and all are deliciously satisfying and low in fat.

Apple and cinnamon cakes with lemon syrup, page 96

Teriyaki beef skewers, page 65

Tomato and cranberry bean soup, page 9

Tuna with char-grilled vegetables, page 35

Eggplant, spinach and butter lettuce salad, page 79

Contents

4

Fast and light – cooking the low-fat way

6

On the table in 30 minutes

52

Prepare ahead

72

Accompaniments

90

Desserts

98

Snacks

106

Breakfast and drinks

Glossary 112

Index 116

Fast and light – the basics

A low-fat diet does not mean a no-fat diet! Indeed, eating a certain amount of fat is absolutely essential for maintaining good health, energy, and glowing skin and hair. However, most of us eat far more fat than we actually *need*, and eating less fat, and less saturated fat in particular, is one of the best things you can do for your health – even if you are not overweight.

The American Heart Association recommends that no more than 25 to 30 per cent of your total daily calories should come from fat, which means about 65g of fat per day for men and 50g for women – and as little as possible of these amounts should be saturated fat (the type found in full cream dairy products, animal fats, coconut, palm oil and chocolate).

How can you eat less fat?

Avoid take out food, as well as commercial cakes and cookies. Eat smaller portions of lean meat and increase your consumption of fish, including canned fish. Always remove the skin from chicken and replace high-fat dairy products with low-fat alternatives. Choose olive or canola oil for cooking (and use it sparingly), and remember that fruit, vegetables, breads and cereals should form the major part of your diet.

But reducing the fat in your diet does *not* mean reducing the flavor. Nor does it mean spending hours in the kitchen concocting special diet food. Our simple tips on these pages – and the fabulous recipes to follow – will help make all your meals healthier and lower in fat, even when you are in a hurry.

Be prepared

A well-stocked pantry, refrigerator and freezer guarantee you will always have the necessary ingredients on hand to put together a healthy, interesting meal without too much effort – and relieve the temptation to resort to high-fat, high-cost take out.

• Garlic, ginger, chiles, fresh and dried herbs, mustard, chutney, lemon juice, soy and teriyaki sauce, Worcestershire sauce, flavored vinegars, oyster sauce, pepper or seasoning mixtures are all essential stand-bys for low-fat flavor hits.

Fresh herbs give food a flavor hit.

Essential equipment

A few basic tools make light work of cooking without added fat.

• Heavy-base, non-stick pans, woks and baking dishes make low-fat cooking easy and cleaning effortless.

• Bamboo or stainless-steel steamers, and the microwave oven, produce great results without added fat, especially with fish and vegetables.

• A cast-iron, ridged grill pan or a barbecue impart a smoky, grilled flavor and create mouth-watering visual appeal – all with a minimum of added fat.

• Baking paper can be used in a variety of ways to eliminate the need for added fat – try lining baking sheets, roasting pans and cake pans, making oiling them unnecessary.

• Cooking-oil spray is a boon when you are trying to reduce added fat – a light spray is all that is needed to prevent food from sticking.

Cooking the low-fat way

• Always *measure* the amount of oil you add to a pan, rather than simply adding a slurp by guesswork.

• Do not even *think* of deep-frying! Instead, roast food in a hot oven on a parchment-paper-lined baking sheet or, if appropriate, steam or microwave food first then crisp in a hot oven after coating lightly with cooking-oil spray. This method produces delicious "baked" potatoes and root vegetables.

• Stir-fry in a wok or non-stick pan rather than shallow-fry.

• Heat your pan or grill before adding oil – it will spread further, so you will need to use less.

• Add the same amount of stock, water, juice, flavored vinegar or wine to pan as an alternative to oil or butter.

• Roast meat on a rack in a roasting pan to allow excess fat to drain away from the meat.

• When slow cooking or stewing, trim all fat from meat and poultry before cooking.

• Prepare casseroles and soups a day ahead and refrigerate so that any fat solidifies on the surface. Skim off all fat before reheating.

• Thicken sauces with pureed vegetables – keep small amounts frozen for the purpose.

Low-fat alternatives

Do not completely deprive yourself – just replace high-fat foods with an appropriate low-fat alternative.

• Instead of ice cream or cream, try whipped chilled evaporated milk (serve immediately) or whipped low-fat ricotta cheese, flavored with powdered sugar.

Whipped low-fat ricotta.

• Use buttermilk or low-fat yogurt in place of sour cream and full-fat yogurt.

• Use filo pastry as an alternative to shortcrust or puff pastry. Coat filo sheets lightly with cooking-oil spray or water, better yet, between layers.

• Instead of oil, use the same amount of stock or water. For salad dressings, use an oil-free variety.

Make salad dressings without oil.

• Make your own reduced-fat version of coconut cream by soaking dried coconut in low-fat milk; let stand for 30 minutes, then strain over a bowl and discard coconut. You can also add a few drops of coconut flavoring to evaporated low-fat skim milk.

• Substitute low-fat margarine or light cream cheese for butter and margarine.

• Always choose a low-fat variety of commercial mayonnaise.

• When selecting cheese, choose low-fat cheddar, mozzarella, bocconcini and ricotta varieties, and remember that a small amount of parmesan cheese (although full-fat) actually gives twice as much flavor as many other cheeses, so you can use less.

• When appropriate, double the cooking quantities and freeze half of the dish for another time.

• Cutting meat or poultry into individual portions, strips or cubes before freezing will save time in meal preparation. Make the package as flat as possible so it will defrost quickly when needed.

Microwave shortcuts

Learn to love your microwave oven and do not use it just for reheating and defrosting. For both fast and low-fat cooking it is invaluable – and cleaning up is a breeze!

• Leftover cooked rice and pasta both freeze well and can be reheated quickly and easily in your microwave oven.

High in fiber, low in fat – microwave popcorn is the ideal snack.

• Microwave popcorn is a low-fat, high-fiber snack. Place 1/4 cup popping corn in a plain paper or oven bag. Secure bag loosely with kitchen string. Place on microwave turntable and cook on MEDIUM-HIGH (70%) for 5 minutes or until popped. Remove bag from oven with tongs and let stand for 2 minutes before opening. Sprinkle with a little salt to serve.

• For tabbouleh in a flash, place 1/2 cup bulghur in a microwave-safe bowl and cover with hot water. Cook, uncovered, on HIGH (100%) for 1 minute. Let stand, covered, 1 minute, then drain bulghur well on paper.

• To make cutting and peeling pumpkin easier, place 1 lb piece of pumpkin on microwave turntable and cook, uncovered, on HIGH (100%) for 2 minutes.

• Corn on the cob tastes freshly picked if you simply place an unhusked cob on the turntable and microwave, uncovered, on HIGH (100%) for about 4 minutes.

• When reheating meals from the fridge, try using a lower heat setting. It may take a little longer, but food will heat up more evenly.

• To cook poppadums without frying, place two at a time on microwave turntable and cook, uncovered, on HIGH (100%) about 30 seconds or until puffed.

Freezer know-how

Many of the recipes in this book are suitable to freeze, or can be made a day ahead, allowing you to prepare ahead for greater time saving.

A baked potato makes a delicious, healthy, light meal.

Precious timesavers

• Use bottled crushed garlic, minced ginger, chopped chile, and so on, rather than starting afresh each time; or freeze appropriate quantities when you have excess.

• Ask the butcher to trim all visible fat and grind your meat purchases for you.

• For a satisfying, low-fat snack, prick a scrubbed, medium-sized baking potato several times and cook, uncovered, on HIGH (100%) for 4 to 5 minutes. Top with an accompaniment, such as low-fat cottage cheese and herbs. If you prefer a crisp skin, place microwaved potato in a hot oven for several minutes until crisp.

FROZEN FOOD STORAGE TIMES

meat and poultry	4 to 6 months
ground meat or poultry	2 months
fish: oily	3 months
white	6 months
shellfish	2 months
fruit and vegetables	6 months
cooked pasta or rice	2 months
cream, cheese, milk	2 to 3 months
butter, margarine	6 months
casseroles, soups, pies	3 months
cakes, cookies, breads	3 to 4 months
eggs (whole, yolks or whites without shell)	6 months

On the table in 30 minutes

You've rushed in late and everyone is *starving*! But you'd still like to serve a healthy, home-cooked meal rather than resorting to take out ... again. Help is at hand. All the mouth-watering meals in this chapter can be cooked and served in half an hour or less, and all are also low in fat – proving once and for all that fast food does not have to be junk food.

Moroccan beef salad with couscous

1 cup vegetable stock
1 1/2 cups couscous
1 lb beef rump steak
1/2 cup dried apricots, sliced
1/2 cup golden raisins
1 medium red onion, sliced thinly
1/4 cup finely chopped fresh mint
3 tablespoons finely chopped fresh dill
1 1/2 tablespoons pine nuts
2 teaspoons cumin seed
3/4 cup oil-free French dressing

Bring stock to boil in large pan; remove from heat. Add couscous to pan, cover, let stand about 5 minutes or until stock is absorbed.

Meanwhile, cook beef on heated oiled grill plate (or broiler or barbecue) until browned both sides and cooked as desired; slice beef thinly.

Fluff couscous with fork, add apricots, raisins, onion and herbs; mix gently.

Place pine nuts and cumin in dry small pan; stir over low heat until seed is just fragrant and pine nuts are toasted. Combine seed and nuts with dressing in small bowl; drizzle over beef and couscous.

SERVES 4
Per serving 14.2g fat; 6.3g fiber; 596 cal.

Minted lamb and vermicelli soup

3 oz bean thread vermicelli
1 1/2 tablespoons peanut oil
1 1/4 lb boneless lamb or sirloin, sliced thinly
2 teaspoons bottled chopped chile
3 tablespoons finely chopped fresh lemon grass
3 tablespoons grated fresh ginger
4 cloves garlic, crushed
1/3 cup fish sauce
6 cups chicken stock
1 1/2 tablespoons sugar
1 lb asparagus, trimmed, chopped
1/4 cup chopped fresh cilantro
1/3 cup chopped fresh mint
8 green onions, chopped finely
4 medium tomatoes, seeded, sliced

Chicken, corn and noodle chowder

1 medium yellow onion, chopped coarsely
2 cloves garlic, crushed
15 oz can corn kernels, drained
2 x 15 oz cans small potatoes, drained, quartered
4 cups chicken stock
12 oz boneless, skinless chicken breast halves, chopped coarsely
5 oz fresh egg noodles
3 tablespoons low-fat sour cream

Heat oiled large pan; cook onion and garlic, stirring, until onion softens. Add corn, potato and stock, bring to boil; simmer, covered, 10 minutes. Blend or process potato mixture, in batches, until smooth. Return potato mixture to same pan, add chicken and noodles; simmer, uncovered, about 10 minutes or until chicken is tender. Serve with sour cream, topped with finely sliced fresh herbs, if desired.

SERVES 4

Per serving 7.5g fat; 5.9g fiber; 351 cal.

Place vermicelli in large heatproof bowl, cover with boiling water, let stand until just tender; drain.

Meanwhile, heat half of the oil in large pan; cook lamb, in batches, until browned all over. Heat remaining oil in same pan; cook chile, lemon grass, ginger and garlic, stirring, until fragrant. Add sauce, stock and sugar; cook, stirring, until mixture boils. Add asparagus; simmer, uncovered, until asparagus is just tender. Add herbs, onion, tomato, vermicelli and lamb; stir until soup is hot.

SERVES 6

Per serving 11.7g fat; 6.2g fiber; 386 cal.

Chicken, corn and noodle chowder *(left)*
Minted lamb and vermicelli soup *(below)*
Tomato and cranberry bean soup *(right)*

Tomato and cranberry bean soup

**2 medium yellow onions,
   chopped coarsely**
2 cloves garlic, crushed
**2 lb plum tomatoes,
   chopped coarsely**
2 cups chicken stock
1¹/₂ tablespoons Worcestershire sauce
**3 tablespoons finely chopped
   fresh parsley**
**2 x 15 oz cans cranberry beans,
   rinsed, drained**

Heat oiled large pan; cook onion and garlic, stirring, until onion softens. Stir in tomato; cook, stirring, about 3 minutes or until tomato softens. Add stock and sauce, bring to boil; simmer, covered, 15 minutes. Blend or process tomato mixture, in batches, until almost smooth. Return tomato mixture to pan, stir in parsley and beans; simmer, uncovered, about 5 minutes or until hot.

SERVES 4

Per serving 0.8g fat; 11.2g fiber; 100 cal.

Fried rice with prawns

Instead of packaged pre-cooked rice, you may wish to cook-ahead 2¹/₂ cups long-grain rice for this recipe. Spread cooked rice on tray, cover with paper towel; refrigerate overnight.

6 dried shiitake mushrooms
1 lb medium uncooked prawns
1¹/₂ tablespoons peanut oil
1 medium yellow onion,
  sliced thinly
1 teaspoon sesame oil
1 clove garlic, crushed
1¹/₂ tablespoons grated fresh ginger
1 medium sweet red bell pepper,
  chopped coarsely
1 medium carrot, sliced thinly
2 stalks celery, sliced
3 oz snow peas
1 lb packet frozen pre-cooked rice
1 cup bean sprouts
6 green onions, sliced thinly
¹/₄ cup oyster sauce
¹/₄ cup hoisin sauce
1¹/₂ tablespoons fish sauce

Place mushrooms in small heatproof bowl, cover with boiling water, let stand 10 minutes; drain. Discard stems; slice caps finely. Shell and devein prawns, leaving tails intact.

Heat half the peanut oil in wok or large pan; stir-fry yellow onion until soft. Add sesame oil, garlic, ginger and prawns, stir-fry until prawns just change color; remove from wok. Heat remaining peanut oil in wok, add bell pepper, carrot, celery and peas, stir-fry until vegetables are just tender. Return prawn mixture to wok with mushroom, rice, sprouts, green onion and sauces; cook, stirring, until hot.

SERVES 4
Per serving 8.2g fat; 7.3g fibre; 367 cal.

Pork, pine nut and cointreau risotto

1 lb pork tenderloin
1¹/₂ tablespoons teriyaki marinade
1 teaspoon finely grated orange rind
3 cloves garlic, crushed
1 large yellow onion, chopped finely
2 cups arborio rice
5 cups chicken stock
¹/₂ cup dry white wine
3 tablespoons Cointreau
5 oz baby spinach leaves
3 tablespoons pine nuts, toasted
3 tablespoons coarsely chopped
  fresh lemon thyme

Place pork on rack in roasting pan; brush with combined marinade and rind. Bake, uncovered, at 450°F 20 minutes. Cover pork, let stand 5 minutes; slice thinly.

Meanwhile, cook garlic and onion in heated, oiled large pan, stirring, until onion softens. Add rice, stock, wine and Cointreau, bring to boil, simmer, covered, 15 minutes, stirring midway through cooking. Remove from heat, let stand, covered, 10 minutes. Gently stir in spinach, pine nuts, thyme and pork.

SERVES 4
Per serving 7.6g fat; 4.9g fibre; 615 cal.

Fried rice with prawns *(left)*
Pork, pine nut and cointreau risotto *(above)*

Mushroom, spinach and lemon risotto

2 medium yellow onions, chopped finely
3 cloves garlic, crushed
1¹/₂ tablespoons finely grated lemon rind
10 oz button mushrooms, halved
2 cups arborio rice
6 cups chicken stock
1 cup dry white wine
10 oz baby spinach leaves
3 tablespoons coarsely chopped fresh lemon thyme

Heat oiled large pan; cook onion, garlic, rind and mushrooms, stirring, until mushrooms are browned lightly. Add rice, stock and wine, bring to boil; simmer, covered, 15 minutes, stirring midway through cooking. Remove from heat; let stand, covered, 10 minutes. Gently stir in spinach and lemon thyme.

SERVES 4

Per serving 1.6g fat; 7.9g fibre; 458 cal.

Tandoori lamb naan

8 oz boneless lamb or sirloin
1¹/₂ tablespoons tandoori paste
³/₄ cup low-fat plain yogurt
4 naan or pitas
3 tablespoons chopped fresh mint
1¹/₂ tablespoons lime juice
3 oz curly endive
1 burpless cucumber, peeled, seeded, sliced finely

Combine lamb, tandoori paste and ¹/₄ cup of the yogurt in medium bowl; cover, refrigerate 10 minutes.

Cook lamb on heated oiled grill pan (or broiler or barbecue) until browned all over and cooked as desired; slice lamb.

Meanwhile, heat naan according to packet directions.

Blend or process remaining yogurt, mint and juice until smooth.

Place lamb, endive, cucumber and yogurt mixture in center of naan; roll to enclose filling.

SERVES 4

Per serving 6.7g fat; 2.2g fibre; 304 cal.

Spicy chicken fried rice

Instead of packaged pre-cooked rice, you may wish to cook-ahead 2 1/2 cups long-grain rice for this recipe. Spread cooked rice on tray, cover with paper towel; refrigerate overnight.

2 teaspoons peanut oil
2 eggs, beaten lightly
1 lb boneless, skinless chicken thighs,
    sliced thinly
2 medium yellow onions,
    chopped finely
1 1/2 tablespoons ground cumin
2 teaspoons ground coriander
1/4 teaspoon cardamom seed
1 teaspoon ground cinnamon
2 small chiles, seeded, chopped finely
2 cloves garlic, crushed
1 large sweet red bell pepper,
    sliced thinly
4 oz fresh baby corn,
    halved lengthwise
1 lb packet frozen pre-cooked rice
4 green onions, sliced finely
3 tablespoons ketjap manis
3 tablespoons coarsely chopped
    fresh cilantro

Heat 1/2 teaspoon of the oil in wok or large pan, add half the egg, swirl so egg forms a thin omelette; cook until set.

Transfer omelette to board, roll, cut into thin strips. Repeat with remaining egg and another 1/2 teaspoon oil. Heat remaining oil in wok; stir-fry chicken and yellow onion, in batches, until chicken is tender. Stir-fry spices, chiles and garlic in wok until fragrant. Add bell pepper and corn; stir-fry until just tender. Return chicken mixture to wok with omelette strips, rice, green onion, ketjap manis and cilantro; stir-fry until hot.

SERVES 4
Per serving 11.9g fat; 6.1g fibre; 451 cal.

Mushroom, spinach and lemon risotto *(above left)*
Tandoori lamb naan *(left)*
Spicy chicken fried rice *(right)*

Easy niçoise-style salad

4 oz green beans
2 x 15 oz cans tuna, drained
1 large red oak leaf lettuce
**15 oz can bite-size potatoes,
    drained, quartered**
8 oz cherry tomatoes, halved
1 cup black olives, pitted
**1/2 cup low-fat French
    dressing**
2 teaspoons stone-ground mustard
1 clove garlic, crushed
2 teaspoons fresh chervil

Place beans in medium heatproof bowl, pour boiling water over beans, let stand 5 minutes; drain. Rinse beans under cold water; drain well. Break tuna into large chunks.

Line large serving bowl with lettuce; top with combined beans, tuna, potato, tomato and olives. Mix dressing with mustard, garlic and chervil in small bowl, pour over salad.

SERVES 6

Per serving 4.2g fat; 3.9g fiber; 202 cal.

Chile prawn and noodle salad

8 oz medium cooked prawns
1/4 cup lime juice
3 tablespoons mild sweet chili sauce
1 small red chile, seeded, sliced
1 small green chile, seeded, sliced
2 teaspoons sugar

7 oz bean thread noodles
**3 tablespoons shredded
    fresh mint**

Shell and devein prawns, leaving tails intact. Combine prawns with juice, sauce, chiles and sugar in large bowl.

Place noodles in large heatproof bowl, cover with boiling water, let stand until tender; drain.

Combine noodles and mint with prawn mixture.

SERVES 4

Per serving 1.4g fat; 1.2g fiber; 212 cal.

Easy niçoise-style salad *(above)*
Chile prawn and noodle salad *(right)*

Warm pasta salad with mustard mayonnaise

We used farfalle for this recipe but any short pasta may be used in its place.

1/2 cup sun-dried tomatoes
8 oz pasta
2/3 cup low-fat mayonnaise
3 tablespoons stone-ground mustard
1 1/2 tablespoons lemon juice
2 cloves garlic, crushed
3 tablespoons hot water
8 oz sliced ham
6 oz baby arugula
2 small red onions, sliced finely
1/4 cup black olives, pitted,
  sliced coarsely

Place tomato in small heatproof bowl, cover with boiling water, let stand about 15 minutes or until softened; drain. Slice tomato thinly.

Meanwhile, cook pasta in large pan of boiling water, uncovered, until just tender; drain. Cover to keep warm.

Combine mayonnaise, mustard, juice, garlic and water in small bowl; mix well.

Cut ham thinly, combine with pasta, tomato, mustard mayonnaise, arugula, onion and olives in bowl; mix gently.

SERVES 4
Per serving 12.8g fat; 6.3g fiber; 436 cal.

Scallop and goat cheese salad

8 slices white bread
12 large scallops
1 medium romaine lettuce
1 small red onion, sliced finely
5 oz hard goat cheese, chopped
6 oz low-fat plain yogurt
1/4 cup lemon juice
1 1/2 tablespoons stone-ground mustard
1 clove garlic, crushed

Discard crusts from bread; cut bread into 1-inch squares. Heat oiled large pan; cook bread, stirring, until browned all over. Remove from pan.

Cook scallops in same pan until browned on both sides and cooked as desired.

Combine bread, scallops, lettuce, onion and cheese in large bowl; drizzle with combined yogurt, juice, mustard and garlic.

SERVES 4

Per serving 13.3g fat; 2.9g fiber; 369 cal.

Warm pasta salad with mustard mayonnaise *(left)*
Scallop and goat cheese salad *(below)*
Sesame chicken noodle salad *(right)*

Sesame chicken noodle salad

1 1/2 lb boneless, skinless chicken
    breast halves, sliced
1 clove garlic, crushed
3 tablespoons mild sweet chili sauce
1/2 teaspoon sesame oil
1/4 cup rice vinegar
3 tablespoons soy sauce
1 1/2 tablespoons lemon juice
1 green onion, sliced finely
2 teaspoons sugar
1 1/4 lb fresh egg noodles
1 medium sweet yellow bell pepper
1 large carrot
6 oz watercress, trimmed
1 1/2 tablespoons peanut oil
8 oz asparagus, trimmed, halved
2 teaspoons white sesame
    seed, toasted

Combine chicken, garlic and chili sauce in large bowl.

For dressing, combine sesame oil, vinegar, soy sauce, juice, onion and sugar in jar; shake well.

Cook noodles in large pan of boiling water, uncovered, until just tender; drain.

Discard seeds and membranes from bell pepper, cut bell pepper and carrot into long thin strips. Combine noodles, bell pepper, carrot and watercress in large serving bowl; mix well.

Heat peanut oil in wok or large pan; stir-fry chicken mixture, in batches, until browned and tender. Add asparagus to wok, stir-fry until just tender.

Combine chicken and asparagus with noodle mixture, drizzle with dressing, sprinkle with seed.

SERVES 6

Per serving 8g fat; 4.1g fiber; 337 cal.

Grilled asparagus, prosciutto and peach salad

3 large peaches
6 slices prosciutto
1 lb asparagus, trimmed
3 tablespoons lemon juice
2 teaspoons extra virgin olive oil
3 oz mizuna

Cut peaches in half, remove seed, cut each half in half again. Cut each slice of prosciutto in half. Wrap peach quarters in prosciutto, place on baking sheet, bake at 450°F about 10 minutes or until prosciutto is crisp.

Meanwhile, cook asparagus on heated oiled grill pan (or broiler or barbecue) until browned and just tender; drizzle with combined lemon juice and oil.

Place mizuna on serving plates, top with lemon-coated asparagus and prosciutto-wrapped peaches.

SERVES 4
Per serving 4.4g fat; 3.8g fiber; 115 cal.

Tuna bean salad

3 oz mixed baby lettuce leaves
15 oz can tuna, drained, flaked
14 oz can lima beans, rinsed, drained
1 small red onion, sliced finely
8 oz yellow pear tomatoes
1/2 cup low-fat Italian dressing
3 tablespoons coarsely chopped
     fresh parsley
3 tablespoons coarsely chopped
     fresh basil

Line 4 serving bowls with mesclun. Combine tuna, beans, onion, tomatoes, dressing, parsley and basil in large bowl; divide among serving bowls.

SERVES 4
Per serving 2.5g fat; 4.3g fiber; 146 cal.

Grilled asparagus, prosciutto and peach salad *(left)*
Tuna bean salad *(right)*

Lamb cracker bread with crunchy chili glaze

1/2 cup mild sweet chili sauce
3 cloves garlic, crushed
1/4 cup beef stock
1/4 cup unsalted roasted peanuts, chopped coarsely
10 oz lamb eye of loin
4 pieces cracker bread
4 romaine lettuce leaves
1 green onion, sliced thinly
1 cup bean sprouts

Combine sauce, garlic, stock and peanuts in small pan; simmer, uncovered, about 5 minutes or until mixture has thickened to a glaze.

Meanwhile, cook lamb in heated oiled medium pan until browned all over and cooked as desired. Remove lamb from pan, cover, let rest 5 minutes; cut into thin slices.

Spread 1 piece cracker bread with a little chili glaze, top with lettuce leaf. Sprinkle 1/4 of the onion and 1/4 of the sprouts across one short end of cracker bread, top with 1/4 of

the sliced lamb, roll cracker bread to enclose filling; cut in half. Repeat process with remaining ingredients. Serve cracker bread with remaining chili glaze.

SERVES 4

Per serving 10.2g fat; 6.1g fiber; 386 cal.

Lamb cracker bread with crunchy chili glaze *(above)*
Rock lobster and raspberry salad *(above right)*
Salmon and dill tortellini salad *(right)*

Rock lobster and raspberry salad

Any type of crustacean (for example, prawns, crabs or lobsters) may be used in place of the rock lobster, if desired.

1 lb small cooked rock lobsters
2 teaspoons olive oil
3 lb watermelon
8 oz arugula
3 oz raspberries
1/3 cup raspberry vinegar
3 tablespoons chopped
    fresh mint
2 small chiles, seeded,
    chopped finely

Cut rock lobsters in half lengthwise, rinse under cold water; drain.

    Heat oil in large pan; cook rock lobsters until heated through and lightly browned.

    Using a 1/2-inch melon baller, scoop watermelon into balls.

    Combine rock lobsters, watermelon, arugula and raspberries in large bowl.

    Mix vinegar with mint and chile in small jar, pour over salad; toss gently.

SERVES 4

Per serving 3.3g fat; 3.6g fiber; 120 cal.

Salmon and dill tortellini salad

You can use a flavored tortellini of your choice. Mild flavors such as ham and cheese or cheese and spinach are the most suitable.

12 oz spinach and ricotta tortellini
1/2 cup low-fat plain yogurt
2 teaspoons stone-ground mustard
1/4 cup oil-free Italian dressing
2 teaspoons finely chopped fresh dill
3 tablespoons water
1 teaspoon sugar
15 oz can red salmon, drained
1 1/2 tablespoons drained capers
2 stalks celery, sliced
1 burpless cucumber, peeled,
    sliced thinly

Cook pasta in large pan of boiling water, uncovered, until just tender; drain. Rinse under cold water; cool.

    Meanwhile, combine yogurt, mustard, dressing, dill, water and sugar in small bowl; whisk until dressing is smooth.

    Combine pasta with flaked salmon, capers, celery and cucumber in large bowl. Just before serving, drizzle with dressing.

SERVES 4

Per serving 10.1g fat; 1.2g fiber; 228 cal.

Chicken and pickled cucumber pita

8 oz boneless, skinless chicken breast halves
1 medium cucumber
1½ tablespoons cider vinegar
2 teaspoons sugar
1 small chile, seeded, chopped finely
1 teaspoon soy sauce
1 small butter lettuce
4 pocket pitas

Cook chicken on heated oiled grill pan (or broiler or barbecue) until browned both sides and cooked through; cool. Slice chicken thinly.

Meanwhile, slice cucumber into long, thin strips with a vegetable peeler. Combine cucumber, vinegar, sugar, chile and sauce in medium bowl; let stand 10 minutes.

Serve chicken, pickled cucumber and lettuce in pitas.

SERVES 4

Per serving 4.7g fat; 3.4g fiber; 321 cal.

Mushroom, eggplant and zucchini pizza

2 medium zucchini
1 Japanese eggplant
6 oz button mushrooms, sliced thinly
2 large pitas
½ cup prepared pizza sauce
½ cup finely grated low-fat cheddar cheese
2 teaspoons finely chopped fresh thyme

Smoked salmon and roasted vegetable cracker bread

2 large sweet red bell peppers
6 Japanese eggplants
4 medium zucchini
4 cracker bread
8 oz arugula
6 oz sliced smoked salmon
1 teaspoon finely grated lemon rind
2 teaspoons lemon juice

Quarter bell peppers, remove and discard seeds and membranes. Roast under broiler, skin-side up, until skin blisters and blackens. Cover bell pepper pieces in plastic or paper for 5 minutes, peel away skin; slice bell pepper thinly.

Meanwhile, slice eggplants and zucchini lengthwise. Place eggplant and zucchini strips, in single layer, on oiled baking sheets. Place under hot broiler or in 450°F oven until lightly browned both sides.

Roll each piece of bread into a cone shape; fill with eggplant, arugula, zucchini, bell pepper and salmon. Sprinkle with rind; drizzle with juice.

SERVES 4
Per serving 5.1g fat; 9.4g fiber; 336 cal.

Chicken and pickled cucumber pita *(far left)*
Mushroom, eggplant and zucchini pizza *(left)*
Smoked salmon and roasted vegetable cracker bread *(below)*

Slice zucchini and eggplant lengthwise. Cook mushroom, zucchini and eggplant, in batches, on heated oiled grill pan (or broiler or barbecue) until browned lightly and just tender.

Place pitas on baking sheet, spread evenly with pizza sauce. Sprinkle 1/4 of the cheese over each pita, top with mushroom, zucchini and eggplant; sprinkle with remaining cheese, then thyme. Bake at 500°F about 10 minutes or until pizzas are browned and crisp.

SERVES 4
Per serving 4.9g fat; 4.4g fiber; 186 cal.

Chicken and tomato omelet

1/2 cup vegetable stock
1/3 cup sun-dried tomatoes
6 oz boneless, skinless chicken breast
   halves, chopped finely
1 medium yellow onion,
   chopped finely
1 clove garlic, crushed
2 eggs, beaten lightly
4 egg whites, beaten lightly
1 1/2 tablespoons finely chopped
   fresh chives

Bring stock to boil in small pan; add tomatoes, simmer, uncovered, about 5 minutes or until tomatoes soften. Drain tomatoes over small heatproof bowl to reserve 1 1/2 tablespoons stock; chop tomatoes.

Combine chicken, reserved stock, onion and garlic in oiled 7-inch sauté pan; cook, stirring, until chicken is browned. Combine tomato, eggs, egg whites and chives in medium bowl, pour over chicken mixture, cook over low heat about 5 minutes or until egg mixture is almost set, tilting pan occasionally. Place omelet under heated broiler for about 3 minutes or until omelet is set and lightly browned on top.

SERVES 2

Per serving 8.2g fat; 1.7g fiber; 234 cal.

Cajun beef roll

1 lb beef rump steak, sliced thinly
1 medium yellow onion,
   sliced thinly
1 medium sweet red bell pepper,
   sliced thinly
3 tablespoons Cajun seasoning
3 medium tomatoes
1 baguette loaf

Heat oiled large pan; cook beef, in batches, until beef is browned and cooked as desired. Add onion, bell pepper and seasoning to same pan; cook, stirring, until onion is browned lightly. Cut each tomato into 8 wedges, add to pan; simmer, uncovered, about 15 minutes or until mixture thickens. Return beef to pan; toss gently to combine with tomato mixture.

Trim ends from bread; quarter loaf then split pieces almost all the way through. Line bread with lettuce leaves, if desired. Divide beef mixture among bread pieces just before serving.

SERVES 4

Per serving 6.1g fat; 6.8g fiber; 387 cal (excluding lettuce).

Chicken and tomato omelet *(above left)*
Cajun beef roll *(left)*
Stir-fried Mexican beef *(right)*

Stir-fried Mexican beef

You can use rib eye, rump, sirloin or top round in this recipe, as desired.

1½ lb beef tenderloin, sliced thinly
1 oz package taco seasoning
1½ tablespoons peanut oil
1 large red onion, sliced thinly
1 medium sweet red bell pepper,
    sliced thinly
1 medium sweet yellow red pepper,
    sliced thinly
4 small tomatoes, seeded, sliced
3 tablespoons fresh cilantro

Combine beef and seasoning in medium bowl. Heat half the oil in wok or large pan; stir-fry beef mixture and onion, in batches, until well browned.

Heat remaining oil in wok, stir-fry bell pepper until just tender.

Return beef mixture to wok with tomato and cilantro; stir-fry until hot.

SERVES 4

Per serving 13.4g fat; 5.9g fiber; 346 cal.

Sweet soy chicken and noodles

8 oz soba noodles
1¹/₂ tablespoons peanut oil
**1¹/₄ lb boneless, skinless chicken
   breast halves, sliced**
7 oz sugar snap peas
3 tablespoons sweet soy sauce
4 green onions, sliced thinly
6 radishes, sliced thinly
**3 tablespoons finely chopped
   fresh cilantro**

Cook noodles in large pan of boiling
water, uncovered, until just tender;
drain. Rinse noodles under hot water;
cover to keep warm.

   Meanwhile, heat half the oil in
wok or large pan; stir-fry chicken, in
batches, until tender. Heat remaining
oil in wok, add peas, stir-fry until
just tender. Return chicken to wok
with sauce, onion and radish; cook,
stirring, until hot.

   Combine noodles and cilantro
in large bowl; serve topped with
chicken mixture.

SERVES 4
Per serving 10.1g fat; 10.1g fiber;
439 cal.

Stir-fried turkey with
lemon and chile

**1 lb boneless, skinless turkey breast,
   sliced thinly**
2 teaspoons finely grated lemon rind
**2 small chiles, seeded,
   chopped finely**
2 teaspoons olive oil
2 cloves garlic, crushed
**1¹/₂ tablespoons finely chopped
   fresh lemon grass**
1 large yellow onion, sliced thinly
1¹/₄ lb fresh ramen noodles
10 oz baby bok choy, chopped
3 tablespoons black bean sauce
¹/₄ cup plum sauce
³/₄ cup chicken stock

Combine turkey, rind and chile in
medium bowl. Heat 1 teaspoon of
the oil in wok or large pan; stir-fry
turkey mixture, in batches, until
browned and tender.

   Heat remaining oil in wok; stir-fry
garlic, lemon grass and onion until
onion is soft. Add noodles and bok
choy; stir-fry until bok choy is just
wilted. Return turkey to wok with
sauces and stock; stir until sauce
boils and thickens slightly.

SERVES 4
Per serving 9.1g fat; 10.1g fiber; 752 cal.

Sweet soy chicken and noodles *(left)*
Stir-fried turkey with lemon and chile *(right)*

Satay pork and noodle stir-fry

1 lb fresh egg noodles
1½ tablespoons vegetable oil
1 lb pork tenderloin, sliced thinly
2 cloves garlic, crushed
8 green onions, sliced thinly
¾ cup beef stock
⅓ cup chunky peanut butter
¼ cup mild sweet chili sauce
2 teaspoons lemon juice
1 lb package fresh Asian-style stir-fry vegetables, thawed

Place noodles in large heatproof bowl, cover with boiling water, let stand until just tender; drain.

Heat half the oil in wok or large pan, stir-fry pork, in batches, until browned. Heat remaining oil in wok, add garlic and onion, stir-fry until soft.

Add stock, peanut butter, sauce and juice, simmer, uncovered, 1 minute. Return pork to wok with vegetables and noodles, cook, stirring, until hot.

SERVES 6
Per serving 12.7g fat; 3.3g fiber; 327 cal.

Stir-fried prawns and noodles

1 lb medium uncooked prawns
6 oz dried rice noodles
1 clove garlic, crushed
3 tablespoons soy sauce
3 tablespoons fish sauce
1 teaspoon sambal oelek
1 cup bean sprouts
¼ cup fresh cilantro

Shell and devein prawns, leaving tails intact.

Place noodles in large heatproof bowl, cover with boiling water, let stand until just tender; drain. Cover to keep warm.

Heat oiled wok or large pan; stir-fry prawns and garlic until prawns are just changed in color. Add noodles, sauces and sambal; gently stir-fry until hot. Stir in sprouts and cilantro.

SERVES 4
Per serving 1g fat; 1.6g fiber; 193 cal.

Chicken chile stir-fry

1 lb boneless, skinless chicken breast halves, sliced
3 small chiles, seeded, sliced
1 clove garlic, crushed
10 oz snow peas
1 large sweet red bell pepper, sliced
¼ cup oyster sauce
3 tablespoons sliced fresh basil
1½ cups bean sprouts

Heat oiled wok or large pan; stir-fry chicken, in batches, until browned and tender. Stir-fry chile, garlic, snow peas and bell pepper until vegetables are tender. Return chicken to wok with remaining ingredients; stir-fry until hot.

SERVES 4
Per serving 3.4g fat; 3.7g fiber; 206 cal.

Satay pork and noodle stir-fry *(above left)*
Chicken chile stir-fry *(below left)*
Stir-fried prawns and noodles *(right)*

Mediterranean-style bell pepper rolls

6 medium sweet yellow bell peppers
1 medium yellow onion,
**   chopped finely**
1 clove garlic, crushed
8 oz asparagus, trimmed,
**   chopped finely**
$1/3$ cup pitted black olives,
**   chopped coarsely**
$1/4$ cup crumbled low-fat
**   feta cheese**
3 tablespoons pumpkin seed,
**   toasted, chopped finely**
$1/2$ cup oil-free
**   French dressing**

Halve bell peppers, remove and discard seeds and membranes. Roast under broiler or in oven at 500°F, skin-side up, until skin blisters and blackens. Cover bell pepper halves in plastic or paper for 5 minutes; peel away skin.

Meanwhile, heat oiled medium pan; cook onion and garlic until onion softens. Add asparagus and olives; cook, stirring, until asparagus is tender. Transfer asparagus mixture to large bowl; stir in cheese and pumpkin seed. Divide asparagus mixture among bell pepper halves, roll peppers around filling; place seam-side down on serving plates; drizzle with dressing. Serve with baby spinach leaves, if desired.

SERVES 4

Per serving 5.9g fat; 4.6g fiber; 140 cal (excluding spinach).

Garbanzos with sweet potato and tomato

$1^1/2$ tablespoons ghee
**   or clarified butter**
2 yellow onions, chopped finely
2 cloves garlic, crushed
2 teaspoons ground cumin
2 teaspoons ground coriander
$1/4$ teaspoon cardamom seed
1 teaspoon chili powder
1 large orange sweet potato,
**   chopped coarsely**
2 cups vegetable stock
$1^1/2$ tablespoons tomato paste
$10^1/2$ oz can garbanzos, rinsed, drained

Crisp green vegetables with tempeh

Fresh tofu may be used in place of the tempeh, if desired.

1 1/2 tablespoons peanut oil
10 oz tempeh, chopped finely
1 lb asparagus, trimmed
1 medium yellow onion,
    sliced thinly
3 cloves garlic, crushed
7 oz sugar snap peas
7 oz baby bok choy, halved
2 1/2 cups bean sprouts
1/4 cup soy sauce
1/4 cup vegetable stock
1/4 cup mirin
3 tablespoons rice vinegar

Heat half the oil in wok or large pan, stir-fry tempeh until browned; remove from wok. Halve asparagus lengthwise.

Heat remaining oil in wok; stir-fry onion and garlic until onion softens. Add asparagus to wok; stir-fry until tender. Add peas and bok choy; stir-fry until bok choy is just wilted. Add sprouts, sauce, stock, mirin and vinegar; stir until sauce boils. Combine tempeh with vegetable mixture in large bowl.

SERVES 4
Per serving 9.6g fat; 9.3g fiber; 194 cal.

Mediterranean-style bell pepper rolls *(far left)*
Garbanzos with sweet potato and tomato *(left)*
Crisp green vegetables with tempeh *(below)*

4 medium tomatoes, peeled,
    seeded, chopped
1/3 cup red lentils, rinsed
3 tablespoons finely chopped
    fresh cilantro

Heat ghee or butter in large pan; cook onion and garlic, stirring, until onion softens. Add spices; stir over heat until fragrant. Add sweet potato, stock, paste, garbanzos, tomato and lentils; simmer, covered, about 15 minutes or until lentils are soft. Stir in cilantro.

Serve with low-fat yogurt, extra cilantro and couscous, if desired.

SERVES 4
Per serving 7.3g fat; 11.1g fiber; 262 cal (excluding serving suggestions).

Thai-style chicken and vegetable curry

3 tablespoons finely chopped
  fresh lemon grass
4 kaffir lime leaves, shredded
1 medium leek, sliced thickly
3 tablespoons Thai-style green
  curry paste
1 lb boneless, skinless chicken breast
  halves, cut into strips
2 x 13 oz cans evaporated
  low-fat milk
4 cups vegetable stock
3 tablespoons soy sauce
4 small zucchini, chopped
10 oz green beans, halved
1/2 small Chinese cabbage, chopped
12 oz choy sum, chopped

Spinach and pumpkin curry

2 lb pumpkin, peeled
1 1/2 tablespoons ghee
  or clarified butter
2 medium yellow onions,
  sliced thinly
2 cloves garlic, crushed
1 teaspoon grated fresh ginger
2 small green chiles, seeded, sliced
1 teaspoon ground coriander
1 teaspoon ground cumin
1 teaspoon black mustard seed
1/2 teaspoon ground turmeric
1 1/2 cups chicken stock
5 oz spinach, chopped coarsely
1/3 cup loosely packed fresh cilantro
1 1/2 tablespoons sliced almonds,
  toasted

Cut pumpkin into 1-inch pieces. Heat ghee or butter in large pan; cook onion, stirring, until browned. Add garlic, ginger, chile and spices; stir over heat until fragrant. Add pumpkin and stock; simmer, covered, about 15 minutes or until pumpkin is tender. Add spinach and cilantro; stir, tossing, until spinach has just wilted.

Just before serving, sprinkle nuts over curry. Serve with steamed rice, if desired.

SERVES 4

Per serving 7.4g fat; 5.3g fiber; 164 cal (excluding rice).

Spinach and pumpkin curry *(above)*
Thai-style chicken and vegetable curry *(right)*
Prawn curry *(far right)*

6 oz baby spinach leaves
1½ teaspoons coconut flavoring
3 tablespoons lime juice
¼ cup coarsely chopped fresh cilantro

Heat oiled large pan; cook lemon grass, lime leaves and leek, stirring, until leek is soft. Add paste; stir until fragrant. Add chicken; cook until browned and tender. Stir in milk, stock and sauce; simmer, uncovered, about 5 minutes or until thickened slightly. Add vegetables; simmer, uncovered, until vegetables are just tender. Stir in flavoring, juice and cilantro.

SERVES 6
Per serving 8.3g fat; 6.5g fiber; 291 cal.

Prawn curry

2 lb medium uncooked prawns
3 tablespoons tikka masala
3 tablespoons mango chutney
⅓ cup vegetable stock
½ cup low-fat plain yogurt
½ cup coarsely chopped
**   fresh cilantro**
2 teaspoons lime juice

Shell and devein prawns, leaving tails intact. Heat tikka masala paste and chutney in large pan; cook prawns, stirring, until just changed in color. Add remaining ingredients; stir until combined.

   Serve with poppadum strips, rice noodles and lime wedges, if desired.

SERVES 4

Per serving 6.3g fat; 0.5g fiber; 206 cal (excluding serving suggestions).

Tuna with char-grilled vegetables

3 medium potatoes
2 medium lemons
2 baby dill pickles,
   sliced thinly
4 small (1¹/₂ lb) tuna steaks
2 teaspoons drained green peppercorns
2 teaspoons drained tiny capers

Boil, steam or microwave potatoes until just tender; cut each potato into 4 slices. Cut each lemon into 6 slices. Cook lemon, potato and pickles, in batches, on heated oiled grill plate (or broiler or barbecue) until browned and just tender; cover to keep warm.

Cook tuna on same grill plate until browned both sides and cooked as desired; cover to keep warm.

Heat peppercorns and capers on same grill plate until hot.

Divide potato among plates, then top with tuna, lemon and cucumber. Sprinkle with peppercorns and capers.

SERVES 4
Per serving 4.7g fat; 4.8g fiber; 290 cal.

Lemony fish fillets with poached leeks

2 medium leeks, sliced thickly
3 cups chicken stock
3 star anise
¹/₂ cup finely chopped fresh
   lemon grass
2 small chiles, seeded,
   chopped finely
3 dried kaffir lime leaves,
   chopped finely
4 medium (1¹/₂ lb) fish fillets
cooking-oil spray

Combine leek, stock and star anise in medium pan, bring to boil; simmer, uncovered, until leek is just tender. Drain over heatproof medium bowl; reserve stock.

Meanwhile, combine lemon grass, chile and leaves in small bowl. Place fish on baking dish, press lemon grass mixture on fish; coat with cooking-oil spray. Bake, uncovered, in 450°F oven about 15 minutes or until fish is cooked as desired.

Serve fish on poached leek; drizzle with a little reheated reserved stock.

SERVES 4
Per serving 9.4g fat; 5.4g fiber; 381 cal.

Tuna with char-grilled vegetables *(left)*
Lemony fish fillets with poached leeks *(right)*

Grilled fish steaks with tangy salsa

2 burpless cucumbers, peeled, seeded, chopped finely

2 radishes, chopped finely

4 medium plum tomatoes, seeded, chopped finely

1 medium sweet yellow bell pepper, seeded, chopped finely

1/2 teaspoon Tabasco sauce

1 1/2 tablespoons sherry vinegar

4 small fish steaks

Combine cucumber, radish, tomato, bell pepper, Tabasco and vinegar in small bowl.

Cook fish on heated oiled grill pan (or broiler or barbecue) until browned both sides and cooked as desired. Serve fish with salsa.

SERVES 4

Per serving 4.8g fat; 2.4g fiber; 208 cal.

Pan-fried fish with white wine sauce

1¹/₂ tablespoons low-fat margarine
1 medium white onion, chopped finely
¹/₃ cup dry white wine
¹/₂ cup half-and-half
**1¹/₂ tablespoons coarsely chopped
   fresh chervil**
1³/₄ lb fish fillets

Melt margarine in small pan; cook onion, stirring, until soft. Add wine; simmer, uncovered, until wine is almost evaporated. Add half-and-half; simmer, uncovered, until sauce thickens slightly. Stir in chervil just before serving.

   Meanwhile, heat oiled large pan; cook fish until browned both sides and cooked as desired. Serve fish and sauce with potato chunks, if desired.

SERVES 4
Per serving 13.8g fat; 0.7g fiber; 325 cal (excluding potato).

Salmon with dill and caper dressing

3 tablespoons low-fat sour cream
1¹/₂ tablespoons drained tiny capers
**2 teaspoons coarsely chopped
   fresh dill**
2 teaspoons cream-style horseradish
1 teaspoon lime juice
4 small salmon fillets

Combine sour cream with capers, dill, horseradish and juice in medium bowl.

   Heat oiled large pan; cook salmon until browned both sides and cooked as desired. Serve salmon with dill and caper dressing.

SERVES 4
Per serving 11.6g fat; 0.4g fiber; 208 cal.

Grilled fish steaks with tangy salsa *(left)*
Pan-fried fish with white
wine sauce *(above right)*
Salmon with dill and caper dressing *(right)*

Pan-fried turkey with garlic and thyme

1¹/₂ lb boneless, skinless turkey breast in ¹/₂-inch slices
1 large yellow onion, sliced
4 cloves garlic, crushed
¹/₄ cup lemon juice
¹/₂ cup evaporated low-fat milk
¹/₂ cup chicken stock
1¹/₂ tablespoons finely chopped fresh thyme
10 oz spinach, chopped coarsely
1 teaspoon cornstarch
1 teaspoon water

Heat oiled large pan; cook turkey, in batches, until browned all over and tender. Add onion, garlic and juice; cook, stirring, until onion is soft. Add milk, stock, thyme, spinach and blended cornstarch and water; cook, stirring, until sauce boils and thickens slightly. Return turkey to pan with any juices; stir until hot.

Serve with mashed potato and steamed vegetables, if desired.

SERVES 6

Per serving 4.7g fat; 2.3g fiber; 186 cal (excluding serving suggestions).

Char-grilled chicken with mango salsa

A 1 lb can of mango slices may be substituted for the fresh mango in this recipe.

4 boneless, skinless chicken breast halves
4 oz spinach, shredded finely
1 medium red onion, chopped finely
1 medium mango, chopped finely
1¹/₂ tablespoons coarsely chopped fresh mint
¹/₄ cup shaved parmesan cheese
¹/₄ cup mild sweet chili sauce

Cook chicken on heated oiled grill pan (or broiler or barbecue) until browned both sides and cooked through.

Meanwhile, combine spinach, onion, mango, mint, cheese and sauce in medium bowl; mix well.

Serve chicken topped with salsa.

SERVES 4

Per serving 6.3g fat; 3.3g fiber; 292 cal.

Pan-fried turkey with garlic and thyme *(above)*
Char-grilled chicken with mango salsa *(right)*

Poached chicken with tropical salsa

2 cups chicken stock
4 boneless, skinless chicken breast
   halves
$1/2$ small papaya, chopped
$1/2$ medium avocado, chopped
1 cup chopped watermelon
$1^1/2$ tablespoons lime juice
2 teaspoons Angostura
   aromatic bitters
2 teaspoons shredded
   fresh mint

Bring chicken stock to boil in large
pan, add chicken; simmer, uncovered,
about 10 minutes or until tender.
Remove chicken, pat dry with paper
towels; cover, refrigerate until cold.
   Slice chicken; top with combined
remaining ingredients.

SERVES 4
Per serving 9.3g fat; 1.9g fiber; 279 cal.

Poached chicken with tropical salsa *(left)*
Chicken with red pesto pasta *(below)*
Ginger, chicken and lime patties *(right)*

Chicken with red pesto pasta

We used sun-dried bell pepper pesto, but any bottled "red" pesto could be used.

4 boneless, skinless chicken breast halves
1/4 cup bottled red pesto
12 oz spaghetti
1 cup fresh breadcrumbs
1/3 cup finely chopped fresh chives
2 teaspoons stone-ground mustard
1/2 cup chicken stock

Coat chicken with half the pesto. Cook chicken on oiled grill pan (or barbecue) until browned both sides and cooked through; cover to keep warm.

Meanwhile, cook spaghetti in large pan of boiling water until just tender; drain. Rinse under cold water; drain.

Heat oiled large pan; cook breadcrumbs, stirring, until browned. Stir in spaghetti with remaining pesto, chives, mustard and stock; cook, stirring, until hot.

Serve spaghetti with sliced chicken, and tomato wedges, if desired.

SERVES 4

Per serving 12.3g fat; 5.4g fiber; 620 cal (excluding tomato wedges).

Ginger, chicken and lime patties

12 oz boneless, skinless chicken breast halves
1 1/2 tablespoons grated lime rind
1 1/2 tablespoons grated fresh ginger
2 teaspoons ground cumin
1 egg white
2 green onions, sliced
1/4 cup all-purpose flour

CHILE SAUCE

2 medium sweet red bell peppers
1 medium yellow onion, chopped finely
4 small chiles, chopped finely
14 1/2 oz can diced tomatoes
1 1/2 tablespoons brown sugar

Blend or process chicken until finely chopped. Add rind, ginger, cumin, egg and onion; process until mixture forms a paste. Using hands, shape mixture into 8 patties, coat in flour; shake away excess flour. Heat oiled large pan; cook patties about 2 minutes each side or until browned. Place patties on baking sheet, bake, uncovered, at 350°F about 15 minutes or until cooked through. Serve with Chile sauce.

Chile sauce Quarter bell peppers, remove and discard seeds and membranes. Roast under broiler or in oven at 500°F, skin-side up, until skin blisters and blackens. Cover bell pepper pieces in plastic or paper for 5 minutes, peel away skin, chop pieces finely. Heat oiled small pan; cook onion and chile, stirring, about 2 minutes or until onion is soft. Stir in tomato and sugar, simmer, uncovered, 5 minutes; stir in bell pepper.

SERVES 4

Per serving 4.3g fat; 3.8g fiber; 215 cal.

Lamb and feta rissoles

12 oz ground lamb
1 small yellow onion,
    chopped finely
1 clove garlic, crushed
1/3 cup pitted black olives, chopped
2 oz low-fat feta cheese, crumbled
1/2 cup fresh breadcrumbs
1 egg white

Combine all ingredients in bowl; mix well. Shape mixture into 8 rissoles.
   Heat oiled large pan; cook rissoles until browned both sides and cooked through.

SERVES 4

Per serving 6.4g fat; 1.1g fiber; 193 cal.

Light 'n' spicy crumbed chicken

2 lb chicken tenderloins or breast
    strips
1/3 cup all-purpose flour
2 egg whites, beaten lightly
1/3 cup packaged breadcrumbs
1/3 cup corn flake crumbs
2 teaspoons garlic salt
1 teaspoon lemon pepper

Toss chicken in flour; shake away excess flour. Coat chicken in egg, then in combined breadcrumbs, salt and pepper. Cover, refrigerate 15 minutes.
   Place chicken in single layer on baking sheet; bake, uncovered, at 450°F about 15 minutes or until cooked through.

SERVES 4

Per serving 10.5g fat; 2g fiber; 448 cal.

Black and white sesame crusted lamb

2 cloves garlic, crushed
1 1/2 tablespoons lemon juice
1 1/2 tablespoons finely chopped
    fresh parsley
2 teaspoons Dijon mustard
1 lb lamb eye of loin
1 1/2 tablespoons white sesame seed
1 1/2 tablespoons black sesame seed

Combine garlic, juice, parsley and mustard in small bowl. Place lamb on wire rack over roasting pan; brush garlic mixture all over lamb, sprinkle with combined seed. Bake lamb, uncovered, at 500°F about 15 minutes or until lamb is browned all over and cooked as desired. Cover lamb, let rest 5 minutes; cut into slices just before serving.

SERVES 4

Per serving 8.3g fat; 1.1g fiber; 194 cal.

Lamb and feta rissoles *(left)*
Light 'n' spicy crumbed chicken *(above right)*
Black and white sesame crusted lamb *(right)*

Pork with tomato relish

**1 medium yellow onion,
  chopped finely**
1 teaspoon ground cardamom
8 medium plum tomatoes, halved
1/4 cup brown sugar
1/4 cup balsamic vinegar
1/4 cup water
4 medium pork rib chops

Heat oiled large pan; cook onion,
stirring, until soft. Add cardamom,
tomato and sugar; cook, stirring, until
sugar dissolves. Add vinegar and water,
bring to boil; simmer, uncovered, about
20 minutes or until mixture thickens.

Meanwhile, cook pork on heated
oiled grill pan (or broiler or barbecue)
until browned both sides and cooked
as desired.

Serve pork with tomato relish, and
pasta, if desired.

SERVES 4

Per serving 13.5g fat; 2.8g fiber; 295 cal
(excluding pasta).

Peanut pork steaks

3 tablespoons peanut butter
3 tablespoons low-fat plain yogurt
2 teaspoons lemon juice
1 clove garlic, crushed
2 teaspoons honey
1 teaspoon ground cumin
6 small pork leg steaks

Combine peanut butter with yogurt, juice, garlic, honey and cumin in small bowl; mix well. Brush pork with peanut butter mixture; cook pork on heated oiled grill pan (or broiler or barbecue) until browned both sides and just tender.

SERVES 6
Per serving 13.5g fat; 1.5g fiber; 241 cal.

Pasta with veal and baby beans

8 oz curly lasagna sheets
1¹/₂ tablespoons olive oil
1 lb veal leg steaks, sliced thinly
1 medium red onion, sliced thinly
10 oz button mushrooms, halved
6 slices prosciutto
8 oz frozen whole baby green beans, thawed
1¹/₂ tablespoons finely chopped fresh sage
¹/₄ cup balsamic vinegar
³/₄ cup chicken stock

Break pasta into 2-inch squares. Cook pasta in large pan of boiling water, uncovered, until just tender; drain. Cover pasta to keep warm.

Meanwhile, heat half the oil in large pan; cook veal and onion, in batches, until browned. Heat remaining oil in pan; cook mushrooms, stirring, until tender. Return veal mixture to pan; add prosciutto, beans, sage, vinegar and stock, stir until hot.

Place pasta in serving bowls, top with veal mixture.

SERVES 4
Per serving 10.1g fat; 7.5g fiber; 471 cal.

Pork with tomato relish *(above left)*
Pasta with veal and baby beans *(left)*
Peanut pork steaks *(right)*

Crusted lamb roast

1¹/₂ lb boneless sirloin roast
1¹/₂ tablespoons stone-ground mustard
2 teaspoons finely chopped
  fresh rosemary
2 teaspoons sea salt

Heat oiled large pan; brown lamb all over. Place lamb on wire rack in roasting pan; brush with mustard, sprinkle with combined rosemary and salt. Bake lamb, uncovered, at 450°F about 20 minutes or until cooked as desired. Cover lamb, let rest 5 minutes; cut into thick slices just before serving.

SERVES 4
Per serving 6.5g fat; 0.2g fiber; 216 cal.

Steaks with bell pepper salsa

1 small sweet red bell pepper,
  chopped finely
1 small sweet green bell pepper,
  chopped finely
1 medium red onion,
  chopped finely
1 large tomato, seeded, chopped finely
1¹/₂ tablespoons chopped
  fresh cilantro
¹/₄ cup oil-free French dressing
2 cloves garlic, crushed
1 teaspoon ground cumin
4 small filet mignon steaks

Combine sweet bell peppers, onion, tomato, cilantro, dressing, garlic and cumin in medium bowl; mix well.

Cook steaks on heated oiled grill pan (or broiler or barbecue) until browned both sides and cooked as desired. Serve with capsicum salsa.

SERVES 4
Per serving 10.1g fat; 2.5g fiber; 261 cal.

Crusted lamb roast *(left)*
Steaks with bell pepper salsa *(right)*

Chicken, lentil and spinach pasta

2 teaspoons vegetable oil
1 small yellow onion, chopped finely
2 cloves garlic, crushed
5 oz ground chicken breast
1/2 cup red lentils
2 3/4 cups chicken stock
3 tablespoons tomato paste
8 oz baby spinach leaves
12 oz shell pasta

Heat oil in medium pan; cook onion and garlic, stirring, until onion softens. Add chicken; cook, stirring, until chicken has changed in color. Stir in lentils, stock and tomato paste; simmer, uncovered, about 10 minutes or until lentils are tender and sauce thickened. Add spinach; stir until spinach is just wilted.

Meanwhile, cook pasta in large pan of boiling water, uncovered, until just tender; drain.

Combine pasta and chicken sauce in large bowl; to mix, toss well.

SERVES 4

Per serving 6g fat; 10.8g fiber; 477 cal.

Pasta with tomatoes, artichokes and olives

2 teaspoons olive oil
1 medium yellow onion,
  chopped finely
2 cloves garlic, crushed
1/4 cup dry white wine
2 x 14 1/2 oz cans tomatoes
3 tablespoons tomato paste
1/2 teaspoon sugar
1/2 cup pitted black olives
14 oz can artichoke hearts,
  drained, quartered
3 tablespoons finely sliced
  fresh basil
12 oz spiral pasta
1/3 cup shaved parmesan cheese

Heat oil in large pan; cook onion and garlic, stirring, until onion softens. Add wine, undrained crushed tomatoes, tomato paste and sugar; simmer, uncovered, about 15 minutes or until sauce is thickened. Add olives, artichokes and basil; stir until hot.

Meanwhile, cook pasta in large pan of boiling water, uncovered, until just tender; drain.

Combine pasta with half the sauce in large bowl; toss well. Serve pasta topped with remaining sauce and cheese.

SERVES 4

Per serving 7g fat; 11.3g fiber; 461 cal.

Pasta with roasted mushrooms and tomato

6 oz flat mushrooms
6 oz button mushrooms
6 oz Italian brown mushrooms
8 oz cherry tomatoes
$1/2$ cup chicken stock
2 teaspoons garlic salt
12 oz fettuccine
$1/4$ cup torn fresh basil
$1/4$ cup coarsely grated parmesan cheese

Cut flat mushrooms into quarters. Combine all mushrooms, tomatoes and stock in baking dish; sprinkle with salt. Bake, uncovered, at 450°F, about 20 minutes or until mushrooms are tender and tomatoes softened.

Meanwhile, cook pasta in large pan of boiling water, uncovered, until just tender; drain.

Gently toss mushroom mixture through pasta; sprinkle with basil and parmesan.

SERVES 4
Per serving 3.7g fat; 7.5g fiber; 398 cal.

Chicken, lentil and spinach pasta *(far left)*
Pasta with roasted mushrooms and tomato *(left)*
Pasta with tomatoes, artichokes and olives *(below)*

Beef with red wine sauce and polenta

4 small filet mignon steaks
3/4 cup dry red wine
1/3 cup red currant jelly
4 cups chicken stock
1 1/2 cups polenta
1/2 cup finely grated parmesan cheese

Heat oiled large pan; cook beef until browned both sides and cooked as desired. Remove beef from pan; cover to keep warm.

Add wine and jelly to same pan; cook, stirring, until sauce thickens slightly. Cover to keep warm.

Meanwhile, bring stock to boil in large pan, add polenta; simmer, stirring, about 5 minutes or until polenta thickens, stir in cheese. Serve beef with red wine sauce and polenta.

SERVES 4

Per serving 14.6g fat; 2.1g fiber; 564 cal.

Pasta with feta and red bell pepper dressing

We used rigatoni in this recipe, but any short, macaroni-type pasta may be used in its place.

13 oz pasta
2 medium tomatoes, seeded, sliced thinly
1 small red onion, sliced thinly
1/4 cup fresh Italian parsley
3 oz low-fat feta cheese

RED BELL PEPPER DRESSING
1 small sweet red bell pepper
1 clove garlic, crushed
1 teaspoon coarsely chopped fresh thyme
1 1/2 tablespoons red wine vinegar
1 1/2 tablespoons lemon juice
1/3 cup vegetable stock

Cook pasta in large pan of boiling water, uncovered, until just tender; drain.

Toss hot pasta with tomato, onion, parsley and red bell pepper dressing in large bowl; sprinkle with crumbled cheese.

Red bell pepper dressing Quarter bell pepper, remove and discard seeds and membranes. Roast under broiler or in oven at 500°F, skin-side up, until skin blisters and blackens. Cover bell pepper pieces in plastic or paper for 5 minutes, peel away skin; chop coarsely. Blend or process bell pepper and remaining ingredients until smooth. Sieve bell pepper dressing into small bowl.

SERVES 4

Per serving 4.6g fat; 6.9g fiber; 403 cal.

Beef with red wine sauce and polenta (left)
Pasta with feta and red
bell pepper dressing (below)

Prepare ahead

With a little foresight and advance preparation, you can take the rush out of rush hour. The recipes in this chapter can all be prepared to near-completion a day or two before needed, then refrigerated. When required, simply add the finishing touches and reheat for a healthy home-cooked meal in minutes – perfect for the family and mid-week entertaining, too.

Hoisin pork kebabs with pancakes

Soak bamboo skewers in water for at least 1 hour before using to prevent them scorching.

1¹/₂ lb pork tenderloin, sliced thinly
¹/₂ cup hoisin sauce
3 tablespoons plum sauce
2 cloves garlic, crushed
1¹/₂ cups all-purpose flour
1¹/₂ teaspoons sugar
³/₄ cup boiling water
2 green onions
1 small green cucumber

Combine pork, sauces and garlic in large bowl, cover; refrigerate at least 3 hours or until required.

Combine flour and sugar in large bowl, add water; stir quickly with wooden spoon until ingredients cling together. Knead dough on floured surface about 10 minutes or until smooth. Wrap dough in plastic; let stand 30 minutes. Divide dough into 16 pieces; roll each piece into a 6-inch round. Heat small frying pan; dry-fry 1 pancake until browned lightly both sides. Repeat with remaining dough.

Keep cooked pancakes covered to prevent drying out. *[Can be made ahead to this stage. Separate pancakes with plastic wrap, seal in plastic bag; refrigerate until required.]*

Thread pork onto 12 skewers. Cook pork kebabs, in batches, on heated oiled grill pan (or broiler or barbecue) until browned all over and cooked as desired. *[If it is necessary to reheat pancakes, remove plastic wrap, wrap in foil, bake at 350°F about 10 minutes or until hot.]*

Meanwhile, finely slice onions diagonally. Halve cucumber lengthwise; peel, discard seeds, slice cucumber finely lengthwise.

Serve kebabs with warm pancakes, onion, cucumber and extra plum sauce, if desired.

SERVES 4

Per serving 5.5g fat; 6.2g fiber; 494 cal (excluding extra sauce).

Pea and ham soup with sourdough croutons

2 thick slices sourdough bread
cooking-oil spray
1¹/₂ lb ham hock
2 cups green split peas
2 medium yellow onions,
**   chopped finely**
2 medium potatoes, chopped coarsely
10 cups cold water
2 cups frozen peas
1 cup water, approximately, extra

Cut bread into large dice. Lightly coat
baking dish with cooking-oil spray, place
bread in baking dish, lightly coat with
cooking-oil spray. Bake, uncovered,
at 450°F, turning occasionally, about
10 minutes or until crisp; cool.
*[Can be made ahead to this stage. Store
cold croutons in an airtight container.]*

Potato lentil patties

2 lb red potatoes
¹/₂ cup red lentils
2 teaspoons olive oil
1 small yellow onion, chopped finely
1 clove garlic, crushed
1 egg, beaten lightly
3 tablespoons finely chopped
**   fresh chives**
1¹/₂ tablespoons finely shredded
**   fresh basil**
¹/₃ cup finely grated
**   parmesan cheese**
¹/₂ cup mild sweet chili sauce

Boil, steam or microwave potatoes until
soft; drain, mash. Meanwhile, place
lentils in large pan of boiling water;
simmer, uncovered, about 8 minutes or
until tender. Drain lentils, rinse under
cold water; drain. Heat oil in small pan;

cook onion and garlic, stirring, until
onion softens. Combine potato, lentils,
onion mixture, egg and herbs in large
bowl; mix well. Using hands, shape
mixture into 12 patties; refrigerate
until firm. *[Can be made ahead to this
stage. Cover, refrigerate until required.]*
   Place patties on parchment-paper-
lined baking sheet; sprinkle with
cheese. Bake at 400°F about 30 minutes
or until browned. Serve with chili sauce,
and salad, if desired.
SERVES 4

Per serving 7.7g fat; 9.6g fiber; 343 cal
(excluding salad).

Potato lentil patties *(above)*
Pea and ham soup with
sourdough croutons *(right)*
Carrot and lentil soup with
caraway toast *(far right)*

Remove and discard rind and fat from hock. Rinse split peas under cold water until water runs clear; drain.

Heat oiled large pan; cook onion, stirring, about 2 minutes or until soft. Add hock, split peas and potato; cook, stirring, 2 minutes. Add water, bring to boil; simmer, covered, skimming surface occasionally, 1$\frac{1}{2}$ hours. *[Can be made ahead to this stage. Cover, refrigerate until required.]*

Remove hock from soup, shred half the ham. Discard hock; keep remaining ham for another purpose. Stir frozen peas into hot soup, cook, covered, about 5 minutes or until peas have softened. Blend or process soup, in batches, until smooth. Return soup to pan, stir in shredded ham and extra water, bring to boil; simmer, covered, 5 minutes.

Serve soup with sourdough croutons.

SERVES 4

Per serving 3.8g fat; 11.5g fiber; 312 cal.

Carrot and lentil soup with caraway toast

4$\frac{1}{2}$ **cups vegetable stock**
2 **large yellow onions, chopped finely**
2 **cloves garlic, crushed**
1$\frac{1}{2}$ **tablespoons ground cumin**
6 **large carrots, chopped coarsely**
2 **stalks celery, chopped coarsely**
2 **cups water**
$\frac{1}{2}$ **cup brown lentils**
8 **slices ciabatta bread**
$\frac{1}{3}$ **cup finely grated parmesan cheese**
2 **cloves garlic, crushed, extra**
1 **teaspoon caraway seed**
3 **tablespoons finely chopped fresh parsley**
$\frac{1}{2}$ **cup buttermilk**

Heat $\frac{1}{2}$ cup of the stock in large pan, add onion, garlic and cumin; cook, stirring, until onion softens. Add carrot and celery; cook, stirring, 5 minutes. Add remaining stock and water, bring to boil; simmer, uncovered, about 20 minutes or until carrot softens. Blend or process soup, in batches, until smooth. Return soup to same pan; add lentils, simmer, uncovered, about 20 minutes or until lentils are tender. *[Can be made ahead to this stage. Cover, refrigerate until required.]*

Place ciabatta, in single layer, on baking sheet; toast under hot broiler until browned. Sprinkle combined cheese, extra garlic, seed and parsley over untoasted sides of ciabatta; grill until topping is browned lightly and cheese is melted. Cut in half.

Stir buttermilk into hot soup; serve with caraway toast.

SERVES 4

Per serving 4.5g fat; 15.9g fiber; 342 cal.

Risotto cakes with basil sauce and pancetta

1/2 cup dry white wine
1 yellow onion, chopped finely
1 clove garlic, crushed
1 cup arborio rice
3 cups chicken stock
3 tablespoons finely chopped
　fresh parsley
3 tablespoons finely chopped
　fresh chives
3 tablespoons finely grated
　parmesan cheese
1 egg white, beaten lightly

2 oz sliced pancetta
1 teaspoon cornstarch
1 teaspoon water
3/4 cup low-fat evaporated milk
1 1/2 tablespoons finely chopped
　fresh basil

Heat 3 tablespoons of the wine in large pan, add onion and garlic; cook, stirring, about 2 minutes or until onion softens. Add rice and remaining wine; cook, stirring, about 3 minutes or until wine is reduced by half. Stir in stock, bring to boil; simmer, covered, 15 minutes, stirring midway through cooking. Remove from heat, stir in parsley, chives and cheese; cool. Stir in egg white. Using hands, shape risotto mixture into 4 patties. [Can be made ahead to this stage. Cover, refrigerate until required.]

Place pancetta on baking sheet, bake, uncovered, at 450°F about 5 minutes or until crisp; drain on paper towels. Break pancetta into pieces.

Heat oiled large pan; cook risotto cakes until browned both sides. Place cakes on baking sheet, bake, uncovered, at 350°F about 10 minutes or until hot.

Meanwhile, blend cornstarch with water in small pan; add milk, stir over heat until mixture boils and thickens slightly, stir in basil.

Drizzle sauce over risotto cakes; top with pancetta.

SERVES 4
Per serving 3.6g fat; 2g fiber; 294 cal.

Gingered prawn and palm sugar rolls

3 lb medium uncooked prawns
1/4 cup grated fresh ginger
3 cloves garlic, crushed
3 tablespoons finely grated
　kaffir lime rind
1/4 cup finely chopped palm sugar
　or brown sugar
1/3 cup mild sweet chili sauce
1/3 cup chicken stock
12 sheets rice paper
48 baby spinach leaves
1/2 cup light soy sauce

Shell and devein prawns; chop roughly. Combine prawns, ginger, garlic, rind and sugar in large bowl, cover; refrigerate at least 3 hours or until required.

Heat oiled large pan; cook prawn mixture, in batches, until prawns have just changed color. Place chili sauce and stock in same pan; simmer, stirring, until sauce boils and thickens, pour over prawns.

Place 1 sheet of rice paper in large heatproof bowl of warm water about 1 minute or until softened slightly. Lift paper from water, place on board, pat dry with paper towels. Repeat with remaining sheets. Place 4 spinach leaves on center of each sheet; top with 3 heaped tablespoons prawn mixture. Fold in top and bottom; roll from side to enclose filling. Serve with soy sauce.

SERVES 4
Per serving 1.9g fat; 2g fiber; 277 cal.

Risotto cakes with basil sauce and pancetta *(left)*
Gingered prawn and palm sugar rolls *(right)*

Polenta with tomato, asparagus and watercress

2 cups low-fat milk
1 cup polenta
1/3 cup finely grated parmesan cheese
1 medium zucchini, sliced finely
2 Japanese eggplants, sliced finely
4 medium tomatoes, chopped coarsely
8 oz asparagus, trimmed,
**   halved lengthwise**
3 oz watercress

Heat milk in medium pan, without boiling. Stir in polenta; cook, stirring, about 10 minutes or until milk is absorbed and polenta is soft, stir in cheese. Spread polenta into oiled 9-inch baking dish, cover; refrigerate until firm. Using 4-inch round cutter, cut polenta into 4 circles. *[Can be made ahead to this stage. Cover, refrigerate until required.]*

Heat oiled medium pan; cook zucchini and eggplant, stirring, until vegetables are tender. Stir in tomato; simmer, uncovered, about 5 minutes or until tomato softens.

Meanwhile, place asparagus on oiled baking sheet; broil until browned lightly and just tender. Place polenta on oiled baking sheet; broil until hot and browned lightly.

Serve polenta with tomato mixture, asparagus and watercress.

SERVES 4

Per serving 3.5g fat; 6.3g fiber; 259 cal.

Gnocchi with caramelized pumpkin and sage sauce

1 lb pumpkin
1/4 cup chicken stock
1 large leek, sliced thinly
1 1/2 tablespoons brown sugar
1 1/2 cups water
2 teaspoons finely chopped
**   fresh sage**
1/2 cup low-fat evaporated milk
2 lb fresh potato gnocchi

Chop pumpkin into 1/2-inch cubes. Place pumpkin in oiled roasting pan; bake, uncovered, at 450°F about 30 minutes or until pumpkin is tender.

Bring stock to boil in large pan, add leek; cook, stirring, until leek softens. Add pumpkin and sugar; cook, stirring,

Eggplant, tomato and leek lasagna

3 medium eggplants
coarse cooking salt
1 large yellow onion, chopped finely
4 cloves garlic, crushed
3 large tomatoes, chopped coarsely
3 tablespoons tomato paste
1/4 cup shredded fresh basil
1 1/2 tablespoons low-fat margarine
2 medium leeks, chopped finely
3 tablespoons sugar
4 large fresh lasagna sheets
1 cup grated low-fat cheddar cheese

Cut eggplants lengthwise into 1/2-inch slices; place slices in colander, sprinkle with salt, let stand 30 minutes. Rinse slices under cold water; drain on paper towels. Cook eggplant, in batches, in heated oiled large pan until softened and browned both sides.

Cook onion and half the garlic in same pan, stirring, until onion softens. Stir in tomatoes, tomato paste and basil; simmer, uncovered, about 20 minutes or until thickened slightly. Blend or process tomato mixture until just combined.

Heat margarine in same pan, add leek and remaining garlic; cook, stirring, until leek is soft. Add sugar; cook, stirring, about 5 minutes or until leek is browned lightly. Cut 1 lasagna sheet to cover bottom of oiled deep 8-inch-square (10-cup) ovenproof dish; place in position. Top with 1/4 of the eggplant, 1/4 of the leek mixture, 1/4 of the tomato mixture and 1/4 of the cheese. Repeat layers 3 times, ending with cheese. Bake, uncovered, at 400°F 50 minutes. *[Can be made ahead to this stage. Cover, refrigerate until required. Reheat at 350°F about 50 minutes.]*

SERVES 6
Per serving 7.4g fat; 8.8g fiber; 218 cal.

about 10 minutes or until pumpkin caramelizes. Stir in water, sage and milk; blend or process pumpkin mixture, in batches, until smooth. *[Can be made ahead to this stage. Cover, refrigerate until required.]* Return pumpkin sauce to same pan; stir over heat until hot.

Meanwhile, cook gnocchi in large pan of boiling water, uncovered, until just tender; drain. Toss hot gnocchi through hot pumpkin sauce.

SERVES 4
Per serving 3.5g fat; 4g fiber; 522 cal.

Polenta with tomato, asparagus
and watercress *(left)*
Gnocchi with caramelized pumpkin
and sage sauce *(above)*
Eggplant, tomato and leek lasagna *(right)*

Herbed chicken kebabs with toasted pecans

Soak bamboo skewers in water for at least 1 hour before using to prevent them scorching.

2 lb boneless, skinless chicken breast halves, sliced thinly
1/2 cup finely chopped fresh chives
1/3 cup finely chopped fresh oregano
1/4 cup finely chopped fresh marjoram
4 cloves garlic, crushed
1 1/2 tablespoons lemon pepper seasoning
3 tablespoons chicken stock
1/4 cup chopped pecans, toasted

Thread chicken onto 12 skewers. Combine chives, oregano, marjoram, garlic, seasoning and stock in shallow baking dish; add chicken skewers, mix well. Cover; refrigerate at least 3 hours or until required.

Cook kebabs, in batches, on heated oiled grill pan (or broiler or barbecue) until browned all over and cooked through. Serve with toasted pecans.

SERVES 6

Per serving 7.8g fat; 1.6g fiber; 231 cal.

Citrus chicken with garbanzo salad

4 boneless, skinless chicken breast halves
1 1/2 tablespoons finely grated lemon rind
1 1/2 tablespoons finely grated lime rind
10 1/2 oz can chickpeas, rinsed, drained
1 medium red onion, chopped finely
2 medium tomatoes, chopped coarsely
1 1/2 tablespoons finely chopped fresh cilantro
1 medium avocado, chopped coarsely
1 1/2 tablespoons lemon juice

Combine chicken, lemon rind and lime rind in medium bowl, cover; refrigerate at least 3 hours or until required.

Combine garbanzos, onion, tomato, cilantro, avocado and lemon juice in medium bowl; mix well.

Cook chicken on heated oiled grill pan (or broiler or barbecue) until chicken is browned both sides and cooked through. Spoon garbanzo salad into serving bowls; top with warm chicken.

SERVES 4

Per serving 14.9g fat; 4.8g fiber; 354 cal.

Chicken and mushroom pastry packets

1 lb boneless, skinless chicken breast halves, sliced thinly
4 oz mushrooms, chopped finely
1 small leek, sliced thinly
¹/₂ cup low-fat sour cream
1¹/₂ tablespoons Dijon mustard
¹/₂ cup grated low-fat cheddar cheese
2 teaspoons finely chopped fresh tarragon
8 sheets filo pastry
cooking-oil spray

Heat oiled large pan; cook chicken, in batches, until lightly browned and cooked through. Place mushrooms in same pan; cook, stirring, until lightly browned and tender. Add leek; cook, stirring, until leek is softened. Return chicken to pan with sour cream, mustard, cheese and tarragon; cook, stirring, until combined. *[Can be made ahead to this stage. Cover, refrigerate until required.]*

Cut pastry sheets in half crosswise; layer 4 halves together, brushing with water between each layer. Repeat with remaining pastry sheets. Place ¹/₄ of chicken mixture on one short end of

pastry; fold in sides, roll to enclose filling. Repeat with remaining chicken mixture and pastry. Place packets on parchment-paper-lined baking sheets, spray with cooking-oil spray; bake, uncovered, at 400°F 10 minutes or until pastry is browned lightly and chicken mixture is hot.

SERVES 4
Per serving 13.8g fat; 2.2g fiber; 377 cal.

Herbed chicken kebabs with
toasted pecans *(above left)*
Citrus chicken with garbanzo salad *(left)*
Chicken and mushroom pastry packets *(above)*

Orange pork medallions with roast vegetables

1¹/₂ lb pork loin medallion steaks
1¹/₂ tablespoons finely grated
  fresh ginger
¹/₄ cup Grand Marnier
2 medium oranges
8 fingerling potatoes
cooking-oil spray
1 medium orange sweet potato
2 medium leeks

Combine pork, ginger and 1¹/₂ tablespoons of the liqueur in large bowl, cover; refrigerate at least 3 hours or until required.

Peel oranges; cut each orange into 4 thick slices. Combine orange slices and remaining liqueur in medium bowl, cover; refrigerate at least 3 hours or until required.

Cut potatoes in half lengthwise; place in oiled baking dish. Coat with cooking-oil spray; bake, uncovered, at 450°F 10 minutes. Cut sweet potato in half crosswise; cut each half into 8 wedges, coat with cooking-oil spray. Add sweet potato to baking dish; bake, uncovered, 20 minutes. Cut leeks in half lengthwise; cut each half crosswise into 4 equal pieces. Add leeks to baking dish; bake, uncovered, about 10 minutes or until all vegetables are browned and tender.

Meanwhile, cook pork on heated oiled grill pan (or broiler or barbecue) about 5 minutes each side or until browned and cooked through; cover to keep warm. Drain orange over medium bowl; reserve liqueur. Cook orange slices, in batches, on same grill plate for 2 minutes each side or until tender.

Serve pork with orange slices and roasted vegetables; drizzle reserved liqueur over orange slices.

SERVES 4
Per serving 4.7g fat; 7.5g fiber; 431 cal.

Pork loin with water chestnut and mushroom filling

1 small yellow onion
1 small chile, seeded, chopped finely
4 oz can water chestnuts, sliced thinly
4 oz fresh shiitake mushrooms,
  sliced thinly
1¹/₂ tablespoons finely chopped
  fresh lemon thyme
2¹/₂ lb boneless pork loin
15 baby spinach leaves

Slice onion into thin rings. Heat oiled large pan; cook onion, chile, chestnuts, mushrooms and thyme, stirring, until chestnuts are browned lightly and onion is soft. Cool for 10 minutes.

Discard rind and fat from pork. Place pork, cut-side up, on board. Make a horizontal cut through the centre of the meaty eye to create a flap; do not cut all the way through. Open out flap, cover pork with spinach, top with water chestnut filling. Roll pork tightly from a long side; tie with kitchen string at 1-inch intervals to make an even shape. *[Can be made ahead to this stage. Cover, refrigerate until required.]* Heat oiled large roasting pan; cook pork, over heat, until pork is browned all over. Transfer dish to 450°F oven; bake pork, uncovered, about 1 hour or until tender.

SERVES 6

Per serving 3.8g fat; 1.8g fiber; 268 cal.

Sourdough, ham and potato bake

6 thick slices sourdough bread
1 cup low-fat milk
15 oz can new potatoes
3 oz sliced leg ham
1/2 cup half-and-half
1/2 cup low-fat milk, extra
1 egg, beaten lightly
2 teaspoons finely chopped fresh sage
1 clove garlic, crushed
1 1/2 tablespoons finely grated parmesan cheese

Cut crusts from bread; discard. Cut bread into large dice. Place bread in large bowl, add milk; let stand 5 minutes.

Lightly oil 9-inch pie dish. Cut potatoes in half. Arrange half the bread over base of prepared dish; top with half the potato and half the ham. Repeat with remaining bread, potato and ham. Pour over combined half-and-half, extra milk, egg, sage and garlic; sprinkle with cheese. Bake, uncovered, at 450°F about 30 minutes or until browned lightly and set. *[Can be made ahead. Cover, refrigerate until required. Reheat at 350°F about 20 minutes or until hot, covering with foil midway through.]*

SERVES 4

Per serving 9.6g fat; 2.2g fiber; 273 cal.

Orange pork medallions with roast vegetables *(left)*
Pork loin with water chestnut and mushroom filling *(above right)*
Sourdough, ham and potato bake *(right)*

Teriyaki beef skewers

Soak bamboo skewers in water for at least 1 hour before using to prevent them scorching.

2 large red onions
1 lb beef rump steak, sliced thinly
1/4 cup teriyaki sauce
1 1/2 tablespoons tomato paste
1 clove garlic, crushed
1 teaspoon brown sugar
2 green onions, sliced finely

Cut red onions in half; cut each half into 6 wedges. Thread onion wedges and beef onto 12 skewers. Combine sauce, tomato paste, garlic and sugar in small bowl; brush sauce mixture over skewers. Cover; refrigerate at least 3 hours or until required.

Cook beef skewers on heated oiled grill pan (or broiler or barbecue) until browned all over and cooked as desired. Serve beef skewers sprinkled with green onion, and steamed rice, if desired.

SERVES 4

Per serving 8.6g fat; 2.7g fiber; 249 cal (excluding rice).

Char-grilled octopus with tomatoes and garbanzos

4 lb baby octopus
3 tablespoons brown sugar
1/4 cup tomato catsup
3 tablespoons barbecue sauce
3 tablespoons Worcestershire sauce
3 tablespoons brown malt vinegar
1 1/2 lb plum tomatoes
3 tablespoons balsamic vinegar
3 tablespoons brown sugar, extra
3 tablespoons water
3 tablespoons finely chopped fresh mint
2 x 10 1/2 oz cans garbanzo beans, rinsed, drained
1/4 cup finely chopped fresh mint, extra
1/4 cup finely chopped fresh cilantro

Discard heads and beaks from octopus; cut octopus in half. Combine octopus, sugar, sauces, catsup and malt vinegar in large bowl; mix well. Cover; refrigerate at least 3 hours or until required.

Halve tomatoes lengthwise. Combine tomato, balsamic vinegar, extra sugar, water and mint in large roasting pan; bake, uncovered, at 350°F about 45 minutes or until tomato is soft. Remove tomato from dish, cover to keep warm. Add garbanzos to pan juices in same dish; simmer, uncovered, about 3 minutes or until mixture is thickened slightly.

Meanwhile, drain octopus; discard marinade. Cook octopus, in batches, on heated oiled grill pan (or broiler or barbecue) until just tender; combine with extra mint and cilantro. Serve octopus with roasted tomatoes and garbanzos.

SERVES 6

Per serving 2.6g fat; 3.4g fiber; 262 cal.

Teriyaki beef skewers *(left)*
Char-grilled octopus with tomatoes and garbanzos *(below)*

Sweet potato and corn frittata

1 medium orange sweet potato
1 fresh corn cob
1 large yellow onion,
  chopped coarsely
1¹/₂ tablespoons demerara sugar
4 eggs, beaten lightly
3 egg whites, beaten lightly
¹/₂ cup low-fat milk
¹/₂ cup grated low-fat
  cheddar cheese

Chop sweet potato into 1-inch pieces. Discard husk, silk and ends from corn cob; cut corn kernels from the cob. Combine sweet potato, onion and sugar in oiled small baking dish; shake dish to coat vegetables with sugar and oil. Bake, uncovered, at 500°F 20 minutes; stir in corn, bake further 20 minutes or until sweet potato and onion are tender. *[Can be made ahead to this stage. Cover, refrigerate until required.]* Combine sweet potato mixture with remaining ingredients in large bowl; mix well.

  Line deep 8-inch-square cake pan with parchment paper. Pour mixture into pan; bake at 350°F about 30 minutes or until frittata is cooked.

SERVES 4
Per serving 9.9g fat; 5.6g fiber; 298 cal.

Chili beans with spicy tortilla crisps

2 medium yellow onions,
  chopped finely
1 clove garlic, crushed
1 medium sweet red bell pepper,
  chopped finely
14¹/₂ oz can red kidney beans,
  rinsed, drained
14 oz can cranberry beans,
  rinsed, drained
28 oz can tomatoes
4 small chiles, seeded, chopped finely
1 cup vegetable stock
3 tablespoons tomato paste
3 tablespoons finely chopped
  fresh cilantro
2 x 7-inch flour tortillas
cooking-oil spray
¹/₂ teaspoon Mexican chili powder
¹/₂ medium avocado, diced

Heat oiled large pan; cook onion and garlic, stirring, until onion softens. Add bell pepper, beans, undrained crushed tomatoes, fresh chiles, stock and tomato paste; simmer, uncovered, about 1 hour or until thickened. Stir in cilantro. *[Can be made ahead to this stage. Cover, refrigerate until required.]*

Cut tortillas into wedges; place on baking sheets. Spray wedges with cooking-oil spray, sprinkle with chili powder; bake, uncovered, at 500°F about 8 minutes or until browned and crisp.

Serve hot chili beans with tortilla crisps and avocado.

SERVES 4

Per serving 10.7g fat; 15.7g fiber; 337 cal.

Roasted red bell pepper tarts

2 medium sweet red bell peppers
2 large yellow onions, sliced thinly
1/4 cup balsamic vinegar
1/4 cup brown sugar
4 sheets filo pastry
cooking-oil spray
3 tablespoons finely chopped
    fresh basil
1/3 cup finely grated parmesan cheese

Quarter bell peppers, remove and discard seeds and membranes. Roast under broiler or in oven at 500°F, skin-side up, until skin blisters and blackens. Cover bell pepper pieces in plastic or paper for 5 minutes; peel away skin. Slice each piece of bell pepper into thin strips. *[Can be made ahead to this stage. Cover, refrigerate until required.]*

Heat small pan; cook onion and vinegar, stirring, about 3 minutes or until onion softens. Stir in sugar; cook, stirring, about 5 minutes or until sugar dissolves and mixture thickens. *[Can be made ahead to this stage. Cover, refrigerate until required.]*

Grease four 5-inch-round quiche pans with removable bottoms. Cut pastry to give sixteen 6-inch squares. Place 1 pastry square in 1 prepared dish, spray with cooking-oil spray, top with another pastry square, placing corners just to the right of previous square's corners. Repeat layering, using 4 pastry squares in each pie dish. Place dishes on baking sheet; bake, uncovered, at 450°F about 5 minutes or until pastry is crisp. Spoon onion mixture into pastry cases, top with bell pepper, sprinkle with basil and cheese. Bake, uncovered, at 450°F about 5 minutes or until hot.

SERVES 4

Per serving 2.6g fat; 2.7g fiber; 159 cal.

Sweet potato and corn frittata *(above left)*
Chili beans with spicy tortilla crisps *(left)*
Roasted red bell pepper tarts *(right)*

Veal rib chops with warm tomato-caper salsa

4 medium veal rib chops
2 cloves garlic, crushed
1¹/₂ tablespoons finely grated
**   lemon rind**
1 clove garlic, crushed, extra
1¹/₂ tablespoons finely grated
**   lemon rind, extra**
2 medium zucchini,
**   chopped coarsely**
3 large tomatoes, chopped coarsely
¹/₄ cup chicken stock
3 tablespoons tomato paste
3 tablespoons chopped fresh oregano
3 tablespoons drained tiny capers

Combine veal with garlic and rind in large bowl, cover; refrigerate at least 3 hours, or until required.

Heat oiled large pan; cook extra garlic and extra rind, stirring, until fragrant. Add zucchini, tomato, stock and tomato paste; simmer, uncovered, until vegetables are tender and salsa is thickened. *[Can be made ahead to this stage. Cover, refrigerate until required.]*

Cook veal on heated oiled grill pan (or broiler or barbecue) until browned both sides and cooked as desired.

Meanwhile, stir oregano and capers into salsa until hot. Serve veal with tomato-caper salsa.

SERVES 4
Per serving 4.5g fat; 4.6g fiber; 229 cal.

Thai beef salad

1 lb beef rump steak
¹/₄ cup lime juice
3 tablespoons shredded
**   fresh mint**
6 oz spinach leaves
2 burpless cucumbers, peeled,
**   seeded, sliced**
1¹/₂ tablespoons white wine vinegar
3 tablespoons fish sauce
1¹/₂ tablespoons brown sugar

Combine beef with juice and mint in medium bowl, cover; refrigerate at least 3 hours or until required.

Heat oiled large pan; cook beef until browned both sides and cooked as desired. Cover beef, let rest 5 minutes; cut into thin slices. Combine beef with spinach and cucumber in large bowl. Gently toss combined vinegar, sauce and sugar through beef salad.

SERVES 4
Per serving 8.6g fat; 2g fiber; 228 cal.

Veal rib chops with warm tomato-caper salsa *(left)*
Thai beef salad *(right)*

Tofu and spinach stir-fry

12 oz firm tofu
1/4 cup hoisin sauce
1/4 cup oyster sauce
1 1/2 tablespoons soy sauce
1 teaspoon finely grated fresh ginger
2 cloves garlic, crushed
2 teaspoons peanut oil
1 large yellow onion, sliced
**1 medium sweet red bell pepper,
    sliced thinly**
7 oz snow peas
12 oz spinach, shredded
1 lb fresh egg noodles

Cut tofu into 1-inch cubes. Combine sauces, ginger and garlic in medium bowl with tofu, cover; refrigerate at least 3 hours or until required.

Heat oil in wok or large pan; stir-fry onion and bell pepper until soft. Add peas, stir-fry until hot. Add spinach, and tofu mixture; stir-fry until hot.

Meanwhile, place noodles in large heatproof bowl, cover with boiling water, let stand until just tender; drain.

Place noodles in bowls, top with tofu and vegetable mixture.

SERVES 4
Per serving 8.9g fat; 8.5g fiber; 356 cal.

Seasoned beef tenderloin

**1 medium yellow onion,
    chopped finely**
3 tablespoons finely chopped walnuts
1/2 cup fresh breadcrumbs
1/2 teaspoon finely grated orange rind
1 1/2 tablespoons dry red wine
1/4 cup stone-ground mustard
3 tablespoons chopped fresh chives
1 lb piece beef tenderloin
1/2 cup orange juice

Heat oiled small pan; cook onion, stirring, until soft. Combine onion, nuts, breadcrumbs, rind, wine, 3 tablespoons of the mustard and chives in small bowl. [Can be made ahead to this stage. Cover, refrigerate until required.]

Cut deep pocket in side of beef, place seasoning in pocket; secure with kitchen string. Heat oiled roasting pan; brown beef all over. Bake beef, uncovered, at 450°F about 25 minutes or until cooked as desired. Remove beef from dish, cover, let rest 5 minutes; slice thickly. Heat same dish, stir in remaining mustard and juice; cook, stirring, until mixture boils. Serve sauce with beef.

SERVES 4
Per serving 11.4g fat; 2g fiber; 269 cal.

Tofu and spinach stir-fry *(left)*
Seasoned beef tenderloin *(right)*

Accompaniments

These accompaniments might be side dishes, but they certainly do not play second fiddle. Indeed, the recipes in this chapter are worth a starring role in their own right – as quick, light meals and snacks, or as part of a vegetarian diet. Easy to prepare, high in fiber and very low in fat – can veggies that look and taste this delicious *really* be good for you as well?

Orange hazelnut beans

1 lb green beans
1/3 cup orange juice
1/4 cup chopped toasted hazelnuts

Boil, steam or microwave beans until just tender; drain. Place beans in large bowl; stir in juice and nuts.

SERVES 4

Per serving 4.8g fat; 4.2g fibre; 333kJ.

Mixed tomato and pumpkin seed salad

4 medium plum tomatoes
8 oz cherry tomatoes
8 oz yellow pear tomatoes
1¹/2 tablespoons pumpkin seed, toasted
3 tablespoons torn fresh basil
¹/2 cup oil-free French dressing

Cut each plum tomato into 6 wedges, combine with cherry tomatoes, pear tomatoes and pumpkin seed in large bowl. Combine basil and dressing in small jar, pour over tomatoes and pumpkin seed; toss gently.

SERVES 4

Per serving 1.5g fat; 3.6g fibre; 53 cal.

Orange hazelnut beans *(left)*
Mixed tomato and pumpkin seed salad *(right)*

Roasted baby vegetables in maple syrup

2 lb new potatoes, halved
14 oz baby carrots, peeled
1 lb baby turnips, peeled
1 lb baby beets, peeled
1¹/₂ tablespoons stone-ground mustard
¹/₃ cup maple syrup
1 teaspoon cracked black pepper
2 cloves garlic, crushed

Boil, steam or microwave potatoes, carrots, turnips and beets, separately, until just tender; drain. Place vegetables in baking dish, pour over combined mustard, syrup, pepper and garlic; shake pan to coat vegetables with maple mixture.
Bake, uncovered, at 500°F about 25 minutes or until vegetables are soft and lightly browned, stirring occasionally.

SERVES 4
Per serving 0.7g fat; 15.3g fiber; 322 cal.

Roasted baby vegetables
in maple syrup *(left)*
Beans and sugar snap peas
with lemon and capers *(center)*
Spiced currant couscous *(right)*

Beans and sugar snap peas with lemon and capers

10 oz lima beans
7 oz sugar snap peas
3 tablespoons drained tiny capers
¹/₄ cup lemon juice
3 tablespoons coarsely chopped fresh dill

Boil, steam or microwave beans and peas, separately, until just tender; drain.
   Heat oiled large pan; cook capers, stirring, until lightly browned. Add juice, peas and beans, stir until vegetables are hot. Stir in dill.

SERVES 4
Per serving 0.6g fat; 3.1g fiber; 40 cal.

Spiced currant couscous

2 teaspoons low-fat margarine
1 medium yellow onion, chopped finely
2 teaspoons ground cumin
2 teaspoons ground turmeric
2 cups water
2 cups couscous
1/2 cup currants
2 teaspoons finely grated lemon rind

Melt margarine in medium pan; add onion,
cook, stirring, until onion is soft. Add cumin
and turmeric, cook, stirring, until fragrant.
Add water, bring to boil; stir in couscous.
Remove from heat, let stand, covered, about
5 minutes or until all water is absorbed,
fluffing with fork occasionally. Gently toss
currants and rind through couscous.

SERVES 4
Per serving 2.7g fat; 5.4g fiber; 400 cal.

Stir-fried Asian greens

1 lb asparagus, trimmed
1 medium yellow onion
1 clove garlic, crushed
7 oz baby bok choy, trimmed
7 oz baby tat soi, trimmed
1¹/₂ tablespoons sweet soy sauce
3 tablespoons water

Cut asparagus in half. Cut onion into thin wedges. Heat oiled wok or large pan; stir-fry onion and garlic until onion is just soft. Add asparagus; stir-fry until almost tender. Add bok choy and tat soi; stir-fry 2 minutes. Stir in combined sauce and water, stir until tat soi is just wilted.

SERVES 4
Per serving 0.4g fat; 3.6g fiber; 38 cal.

Roasted bell pepper and olive salad

2 large sweet red bell peppers
2 large sweet green bell peppers
2 large sweet yellow bell peppers
¹/₃ cup black olives, pitted
1¹/₂ tablespoons balsamic vinegar

Quarter each of the bell peppers, remove and discard seeds and membranes. Roast under broiler or in oven at 500°F, skin-side up, until skin blisters and blackens. Cover bell pepper pieces in plastic or paper for 5 minutes, peel away skin and discard. Combine bell pepper quarters with olives and vinegar in medium bowl.

SERVES 4
Per serving 1.2g fat; 5.5g fiber; 111 cal.

Two-mushroom salad

10 oz Italian brown mushrooms
10 oz button mushrooms
5 oz mixed baby lettuce leaves
1/4 cup lemon juice
1 1/2 tablespoons stone-ground mustard
1 1/2 tablespoons chopped fresh thyme

Cook Italian brown and button mushrooms, in batches, on heated oiled grill pan (or broiler or barbecue) until browned and just tender. Combine lettuce leaves and mushrooms in large bowl, pour over combined juice, mustard and thyme; toss gently.

SERVES 4

Per serving 0.7g fat; 4.7g fiber; 45 cal.

Garlic fingerling potatoes

2 lb fingerling potatoes
8 cloves garlic
1 teaspoon salt

Boil, steam or microwave potatoes until just tender; drain. Cut potatoes in half lengthwise, place in oiled baking dish with garlic; sprinkle with salt.
Bake, uncovered, at 450°F about 45 minutes or until potato is brown and crisp. Squeeze 2 of the garlic cloves over potato; shake gently to combine.

SERVES 4

Per serving 0.4g fat; 5g fiber; 169 cal.

Stir-fried Asian greens *(far left)*
Roasted bell pepper and olive salad *(back)*
Two-mushroom salad *(far right)*
Garlic fingerling potatoes *(front)*

Eggplant, spinach and butter lettuce salad

1 small eggplant, sliced thinly
5 oz baby spinach leaves
1 small butter lettuce
2 burpless cucumbers, peeled,
   seeded, sliced finely
2 green onions, sliced finely
1/2 cup oil-free Italian dressing

Place eggplant, in single layer, on baking sheet; broil until lightly browned on both sides. Combine eggplant with spinach, torn lettuce leaves, cucumber, onion and dressing in large bowl.

SERVES 4

Per serving 0.5g fat; 4.4g fiber; 42 cal.

Red lentil salad

Lentils can be used warm, or leave to cool before assembling salad.

1 1/2 cups red lentils
2 teaspoons cumin seed
2 teaspoons ground coriander
4 green onions, sliced finely
1 clove garlic, crushed
1/4 cup lime juice
1/4 cup seasoned rice vinegar
1/4 cup finely chopped
   fresh cilantro

Cover lentils with water in medium pan, bring to boil, then simmer, covered, about 10 minutes or until lentils are just tender; drain.
   Heat small pan, cook seed and ground coriander, stirring, until fragrant.
   Combine lentils with onion, garlic, spices, lime juice, vinegar and fresh cilantro in large bowl; mix well.

SERVES 4

Per serving 1.9g fat; 11.5g fiber; 213 cal.

Brandied carrots and leek

1 large leek
3 large carrots
1/4 cup water
1/4 cup brandy
3 tablespoons honey

Cut leek and carrots into 4-inch lengths. Heat the water in large pan; cook carrot, covered, about 5 minutes or until carrot is just tender, stirring occasionally. Add leek, cook, stirring, until leek is tender. Add brandy and honey, stir over heat until sauce is syrupy.

SERVES 4

Per serving 0.4g fat; 6.7g fiber; 120 cal.

Eggplant, spinach and butter lettuce salad *(left)*
Red lentil salad *(above right)*
Brandied carrots and leek *(right)*

Low-fat caesar-style salad

1 ciabatta loaf
5 oz sliced ham, chopped finely
$^1/_2$ cup buttermilk
1$^1/_2$ tablespoons lemon juice
1$^1/_2$ tablespoons Dijon mustard
1 clove garlic, crushed
1 medium romaine lettuce
2 medium plum tomatoes, quartered
1 burpless cucumber, peeled,
   sliced thinly

Remove and discard crust from bread, slice bread into 1-inch-thick slices; cut slices into 1$^1/_2$-inch squares. Place squares, in single layer, on baking sheet. Bake at 500°F about 10 minutes or until croutons are lightly browned, turning occasionally; cool.

Heat large pan; cook ham, stirring, until lightly browned.

Combine buttermilk, juice, mustard and garlic in small jar.

Combine torn lettuce leaves with croutons, tomato, cucumber and ham in large bowl, pour buttermilk dressing over salad; mix gently.

SERVES 4

Per serving 4.1g fat; 7.5g fiber; 290 cal.

Smoky potato salad

2 lb new potatoes, halved
7 oz sliced ham
2 cloves garlic, crushed
3 tablespoons cider vinegar
1$^1/_2$ tablespoons stone-ground mustard
2 teaspoons olive oil
1$^1/_2$ tablespoons finely chopped
   fresh chives
2 green onions, chopped finely

Boil, steam or microwave potato until just tender; drain. Cook potato, in batches, on heated oiled grill pan (or broiler or barbecue) until browned all over. Cook ham, in batches, on heated oiled grill pan until browned both sides; chop coarsely. Combine garlic, vinegar, mustard, oil and chives in jar; shake well. Combine potato and ham in large bowl; pour dressing over salad, sprinkle with onions.

SERVES 4

Per serving 6.4g fat; 4.9g fiber; 251 cal.

Green pea puree

$^1/_2$ cup dry white wine
1 medium yellow onion,
   chopped finely
$^1/_2$ cup chicken stock
1 lb frozen peas
1$^1/_2$ tablespoons finely chopped
   fresh mint

Heat wine in medium pan, add onion, cook, stirring, about 5 minutes or until onion is soft and wine reduced by half. Stir in chicken stock and peas, bring to boil, then simmer, uncovered, about 10 minutes or until peas are soft. Stir in mint. Blend or process pea mixture, in batches, until smooth.

SERVES 4

Per serving 0.6g fat; 7.9g fiber; 94 cal.

Low-fat caesar-style salad *(left)*
Smoky potato salad *(center)*
Green pea puree *(right)*

Zucchini, squash and fava bean medley

1¹/₂ tablespoons low-fat margarine, melted
1 teaspoon finely grated lemon rind
1¹/₂ tablespoons lemon juice
3 tablespoons stone-ground mustard
3 tablespoons finely chopped fresh parsley
2 large zucchini
14 oz yellow squash, quartered
1 lb frozen fava beans

For dressing, combine margarine, rind, juice, mustard and parsley in small bowl.

Cut zucchini into ¹/₂-inch-wide slices. Boil, steam or microwave squash, zucchini and beans, separately, until tender; drain. Combine hot vegetables with half the dressing in large bowl; drizzle with remaining dressing.

SERVES 4

Per serving 3g fat; 11.2g fiber; 111 cal.

Coleslaw with fat-free dressing

We used crinkly savoy cabbage for this recipe.

1/2 small cabbage, sliced finely
1 large carrot, grated coarsely
4 green onions, sliced thinly
2 stalks celery, sliced thinly
1/4 cup white wine vinegar
3 tablespoons stone-ground mustard

Combine cabbage, carrot, onion and celery in large bowl. Combine vinegar and mustard in small bowl, pour over vegetables; toss well.

SERVES 4

Per serving 0.6g fat; 7.9g fiber; 54 cal.

Long bean and asparagus salad with citrus dressing

1 lb asparagus, trimmed
7 oz long beans, trimmed
2 small tomatoes, chopped finely
1 small red onion, chopped finely
2 cloves garlic, crushed
1 1/2 tablespoons lemon juice
3 tablespoons orange juice
1 1/2 tablespoons cider vinegar

Slice asparagus and beans into 2-inch lengths. Place asparagus in large pan of boiling water; drain immediately. Place beans in large pan of boiling water; drain immediately. Combine asparagus, beans, tomato and onion in large bowl. Combine garlic, juices and vinegar in small jar; pour dressing over salad just before serving.

SERVES 4

Per serving 0.4g fat; 4.1g fiber; 47 cal.

Zucchini, squash and fava bean medley *(left)*
Coleslaw with fat-free dressing *(center)*
Long bean and asparagus salad with citrus dressing *(right)*

Potato crisps

4 medium potatoes
cooking-oil spray

Slice unpeeled potato thinly, rinse well, pat dry with paper towels. Line baking sheets with parchment paper, place slices, in single layer, on sheets; spray with oil. Bake at 450°F about 20 minutes or until crisps are browned and crunchy.

SERVES 4

Per serving 0.1g fat; 1.7g fiber; 70 cal.

Potato crisps *(left)*
Crunchy baked rosti *(center left)*
Potato cakes *(center right)*
Mixed vegetables with honey glaze *(right)*

Potato cakes

2 lb potatoes, peeled
1 clove garlic, crushed
1 teaspoon lemon pepper seasoning
¹/₂ cup finely grated low-fat cheddar cheese
3 tablespoons low-fat sour cream

Boil, steam or microwave potato until just tender; drain. Mash potato; combine with remaining ingredients in large bowl, cool. Using hands, shape 1/3 cup of mixture into a patty; repeat with remaining mixture. Cook patties, in batches, in heated oiled large pan until lightly browned both sides and heated through.

SERVES 4

Per serving 5.9g fat; 4.3g fiber; 236 cal.

Mixed vegetables with honey glaze

14 oz baby carrots
7 oz sugar snap peas
4 oz baby corn, halved
1 1/2 tablespoons low-fat margarine
1/4 cup orange juice
3 tablespoons honey

Boil, steam or microwave carrot, peas and corn, separately, until just tender; drain. Melt margarine in large pan; add carrot, peas, corn, juice and honey, stir until vegetables are hot and glaze is syrupy.

SERVES 4

Per serving 2.5g fat; 5.4g fiber; 133 cal.

Crunchy baked rosti

2 medium potatoes, peeled
1 teaspoon low-fat margarine
1 medium leek, sliced thinly
2 cloves garlic, crushed
1/2 teaspoon mild paprika
1/4 cup finely grated parmesan cheese

Boil, steam or microwave potato until just tender; drain, cool. Coarsely grate potato. Melt margarine in large pan; cook leek, garlic and paprika, stirring, until leek is lightly browned.

Combine leek mixture, potato and cheese in medium bowl. Place 3-inch egg ring on parchment-paper-covered baking sheet, press 1/4 cup of potato mixture into ring; gently remove ring. Repeat with remaining potato mixture. Bake at 500°F about 20 minutes or until browned.

SERVES 4

Per serving 2.5g fat; 3.5g fiber; 107 cal.

Feta, olive and arugula salad with roasted tomatoes

6 medium plum tomatoes
3 tablespoons brown sugar
3 tablespoons balsamic vinegar
2 teaspoons Dijon mustard
1¹/₂ tablespoons brown sugar, extra
8 oz baby arugula
1 large red onion, chopped finely
¹/₃ cup black olives, pitted, sliced finely
2 oz low-fat feta cheese, crumbled

Cut tomatoes in half lengthwise. Place tomatoes, cut-side up, on baking sheet, sprinkle with sugar. Bake, uncovered, at 450°F about 10 minutes or until just tender.

For dressing, combine vinegar, mustard and extra sugar in small jar.

Just before serving, combine arugula, onion, olives and tomato in large bowl, drizzle dressing over salad, sprinkle with cheese.

SERVES 4

Per serving 2.9g fat; 4.3g fiber; 135 cal.

White beans in rich tomato sauce

1 medium yellow onion, chopped finely
2 cloves garlic, crushed
14¹/₂ oz can tomato puree
2 x 14 oz cans cannellini beans, rinsed, drained
1¹/₂ tablespoons finely chopped Italian parsley

Heat oiled medium pan, add onion and garlic, cook, stirring, until onion is soft. Stir in tomato puree and beans, simmer, uncovered, until thickened slightly. Stir in parsley.

SERVES 4

Per serving 1g fat; 11g fiber; 133 cal.

Pumpkin and parsnip bake

1¹/₂ lb pumpkin
2 large parsnips
1 clove garlic, crushed
cooking-oil spray
1¹/₂ tablespoons low-fat margarine, melted
1 cup fresh breadcrumbs

Peel pumpkin, discard seeds, cut pumpkin into large dice. Peel parsnips; cut parsnips into large dice. Combine pumpkin, parsnip and garlic in large baking dish, lightly coat vegetables with cooking-oil spray. Bake, uncovered, at 450°F about 30 minutes or until vegetables are lightly browned and tender. Sprinkle with combined margarine and breadcrumbs; toss through gently. Bake about 10 minutes or until breadcrumbs are golden brown.

SERVES 4

Per serving 3.3g fat; 4.7g fiber; 168 cal.

Feta, olive and arugula salad with roasted tomatoes *(above left)*
White beans in rich tomato sauce *(left)*
Pumpkin and parsnip bake *(right)*

Bacon, buttermilk and chive puree

2 slices bacon
4 large potatoes, halved
1/2 cup buttermilk
3 tablespoons finely chopped
   fresh chives

Discard fat from bacon, chop bacon finely. Heat small pan, cook bacon, stirring, until crisp; drain on paper towels.

Meanwhile, boil, steam or microwave potato until just tender; drain. Push potato through sieve into large bowl; stir in bacon, buttermilk and chives.

SERVES 4

Per serving 3.4g fat; 5.8g fiber; 278 cal.

Bacon, buttermilk and chive puree *(below left)*
Tomato and basil potatoes *(below right)*
Wild rice salad *(right)*

Tomato and basil potatoes

2 lb new potatoes, halved
cooking-oil spray
1 medium yellow onion, sliced thinly
2 cloves garlic, crushed
2 medium tomatoes, seeded,
   sliced thinly
1 1/2 tablespoons white wine vinegar
3/4 cup tomato juice
1/2 teaspoon sugar
3 tablespoons chopped fresh basil

Boil, steam or microwave potato until just tender; drain. Place potato in baking dish, spray with cooking-oil spray, bake, uncovered, at 450°F about 30 minutes or until lightly browned.

Just before serving, cook onion in large pan, stirring, until soft. Add garlic, tomato, vinegar, juice and sugar, bring to boil, then simmer, uncovered, about 5 minutes or until sauce thickens. Combine potato with tomato mixture in large bowl; mix in basil.

SERVES 4

Per serving 0.4g fat; 6.4g fiber; 193 cal.

Wild rice salad

1 cup wild rice
2 cups brown rice
2 stalks celery, sliced finely
11 oz can corn, drained
4 medium tomatoes, seeded,
   sliced thinly
2/3 cup oil-free French dressing
2 cloves garlic, crushed
1/3 cup finely chopped fresh
   Italian parsley

Cook wild rice in large pan of boiling water, uncovered, until just tender; drain. Rinse under cold water; drain.

Meanwhile, cook brown rice in another large pan of boiling water, uncovered, until just tender; drain. Rinse under cold water; drain.

Combine wild rice and brown rice in large bowl with celery, corn and tomato. Add combined dressing, garlic and parsley; mix well.

SERVES 6

Per serving 2.9g fat; 2.1g fiber; 406 cal.

Desserts

Go on, indulge yourself a little. These dazzling desserts – some ready in minutes, others suitable to prepare ahead – will satisfy the sweetest tooth without adding to your waistline. Fruit features, of course, but there are also creamy mousses and yogurts, melt-in-the-mouth meringues, delectable pastries and even – bliss! – a touch of chocolate.

Vanilla ricotta mousse

Can be partially prepared ahead.

3^1/$_2$ oz low-fat ricotta cheese
8 oz low-fat vanilla yogurt
^{1}/$_2$ cup superfine sugar
1 teaspoon vanilla extract
1 teaspoon gelatin
^{1}/$_2$ cup water
1 cup sweet dessert wine
1 vanilla bean, split

Lightly grease four ^{1}/$_2$-cup shallow dishes. Blend or process ricotta, yogurt, 1^1/$_2$ tablespoons of the sugar and vanilla until smooth. Sprinkle gelatin over 1^1/$_2$ tablespoons of the water in cup, set cup in pan of simmering water, stir until gelatin is dissolved. Stir gelatin through ricotta mixture, pour evenly into prepared dishes, cover; refrigerate about 30 minutes or until set. *[Can be kept in refrigerator up to 2 days.]*

Combine remaining sugar, remaining water, wine and vanilla bean in small pan; stir over heat, without boiling, until sugar dissolves. Bring to boil; simmer about 5 minutes or until syrup thickens. Remove and discard bean; let syrup cool.

Just before serving, turn mousse onto plates; serve with wine syrup.

SERVES 4

Per serve 2.2g fat; 0.02g fiber; 235 cal.

French meringues with berries

Can be partially prepared ahead.

2 egg whites
1 teaspoon lemon juice
^{1}/$_2$ cup superfine sugar
^{1}/$_3$ cup shelled pistachios, chopped finely
7 oz low-fat strawberry yogurt
3 oz fresh raspberries
3 oz fresh blueberries

Beat egg whites and juice in small bowl with electric mixer until soft peaks form. Add sugar, in batches, beating until dissolved between additions.

Line 3 baking sheets with parchment paper, trace twelve 2-inch circles onto each sheet of baking paper. Spread meringue thinly over circles on paper, sprinkle with nuts; bake at 250°F about 30 minutes or until crisp. Cool in oven with door ajar. *[Can be made ahead to this stage. Store in airtight container up to 3 days.]*

Divide yogurt among 18 of the meringues, decorate with raspberries and blueberries; top with remaining meringues. Decorate with extra berries, if desired.

MAKES 18

Per meringue 0.7g fat; 0.3g fiber; 27 cal (excluding extra berries).

Vanilla ricotta mousse *(left)*
French meringues with berries *(right)*

Lime and lemon grass mangoes

2 cups sugar
2 cups water
1¹/₂ tablespoons finely grated lime rind
¹/₄ cup lime juice
4-inch piece fresh lemon grass, sliced finely
2 kaffir lime leaves, sliced finely
4 large mangoes

Combine sugar, water, rind, juice, lemon grass and lime leaves in medium pan; stir, over low heat, until sugar dissolves. Bring to boil; simmer, uncovered, about 15 minutes or until syrup has thickened slightly.

Meanwhile, cut through mango lengthwise, on each side of seed, to give 2 cheeks; peel away skin. Place mango cheeks in large heatproof bowl; pour syrup over mango, serving warm or cold.

SERVES 4

Per serving 0.9g fat; 6.5g fiber; 666 cal.

Grilled Asian pears with rosewater syrup

2 cups water
³/₄ cup superfine sugar
2¹/₂ teaspoons rosewater
4 medium Asian pears, halved
1¹/₂ tablespoons honey
1¹/₂ tablespoons brown sugar

Combine water, superfine sugar and rosewater in medium pan; stir over heat, without boiling, until sugar dissolves. Add pears; simmer, uncovered, about 10 minutes or until pears are tender.

Drain pears over large heatproof bowl; reserve syrup, cover to keep warm. Place pears on baking sheet, drizzle with honey, sprinkle with brown sugar. Broil pears until sugar dissolves. Serve pears warm or cold with warm rosewater syrup.

SERVES 4

Per serving 0.3g fat; 5.8g fiber; 320 cal.

Fresh fruit with passion fruit yogurt

You will need about 2 passion fruit for this recipe.

1/4 medium cantaloupe
1/2 medium pineapple
4 medium plums
4 medium fresh figs, sliced
7 oz low-fat plain yogurt
3 tablespoons passion fruit pulp
1/4 cup honey

Chop cantaloupe, pineapple and plums into bite-size pieces; place in serving bowls. Add fig, top with yogurt; drizzle with passion fruit and honey.

SERVES 4
Per serving 1.3g fat; 7.3g fiber; 201 cal.

Raspberries and watermelon with hazelnut syrup

Use fresh or frozen raspberries in this recipe.

3 lb watermelon
5 oz raspberries
1/4 cup shredded fresh mint
1/2 cup lemon juice
3 tablespoons demerara sugar
1/3 cup coarsely chopped toasted hazelnuts

Discard watermelon rind; chop watermelon into large pieces. Combine watermelon, raspberries and mint in large heatproof bowl.

Combine juice, sugar and nuts in small pan; stir, over low heat, until sugar is dissolved. Bring to boil. Pour hot syrup over watermelon mixture.

SERVES 4
Per serving 6.8g fat; 4.7g fiber; 170 cal.

Lime and lemon grass mangoes *(above left)*
Grilled Asian pears with rosewater syrup *(left)*
Fresh fruit with passion fruit yogurt *(above right)*
Raspberries and watermelon with
hazelnut syrup *(right)*

Fruit with creamy chocolate dip

Tia Maria is a coffee-flavored liqueur; you can use Kahlua as a substitute.

8 oz cottage cheese
7 oz low-fat vanilla yogurt
2 teaspoons cocoa powder
1/2 cup firmly packed brown sugar
3 tablespoons Tia Maria
8 oz strawberries
2 large bananas
2 large red apples

Blend or process cheese, yogurt, cocoa, sugar and liqueur until smooth. Spoon into serving bowl, cover; refrigerate 30 minutes.

Just before serving, cut strawberries in half; slice bananas and apples into bite-size pieces. Serve fruit with dip.

SERVES 4

Per serving 6.5g fat; 5.2g fiber; 379 cal.

Chocolate and ice cream filo sandwiches

4 sheets filo pastry
cooking-oil spray
1 egg white, beaten lightly
1 1/2 tablespoons shelled pistachios, chopped finely
2 teaspoons superfine sugar
1/4 teaspoon ground cinnamon
14 oz low-fat vanilla ice cream
1/2 cup diet chocolate topping

Stack filo sheets together, spraying between each layer with cooking-oil spray. Cut filo stack in half lengthwise, then cut each half into quarters crosswise; you will have 8 rectangular filo stacks in all. Place stacks on greased baking sheets. Brush 4 stacks with egg white, sprinkle with nuts, then combined sugar and cinnamon. Bake all stacks at 450°F about 5 minutes or until golden brown and crisp.

Just before serving, place 1 plain stack on each plate, top with scoops of ice cream, drizzle with topping; sandwich with remaining stacks.

SERVES 4

Per serving 5.1g fat; 0.6g fiber; 88 cal.

Fruit with creamy chocolate dip *(above left)*
Chocolate and ice cream filo sandwiches *(left)*
Watermelon mint ice *(above right)*
Sparkling lime granita *(below right)*

Sparkling lime granita

Can be partially prepared ahead. You will need about 6 large limes for this recipe; grate rind before squeezing juice. We used a sparkling chardonnay for this recipe, but any sparkling white wine may be used.

1/2 cup superfine sugar
1/4 cup water
1/2 cup fresh lime juice
2 cups sparkling white wine
3 tablespoons finely grated lime rind
1 egg white, beaten lightly

Combine sugar, water and juice in small pan; cook, stirring, over low heat until sugar dissolves. Bring to boil; simmer, uncovered, 5 minutes. Stir in wine and rind. Pour mixture into loaf pan, cover with foil; freeze until just firm. *[Can be frozen up to 2 days.]*

Chop mixture, place in large bowl of electric mixer; beat in egg white until combined. Return to pan, cover; freeze until firm.

SERVES 4

Per serving 0.07g fat; 0.2g fiber; 202 cal.

Watermelon mint ice

Can be prepared ahead.

3 lb watermelon
1/2 cup superfine sugar
1 cup water
1/4 cup coarsely chopped fresh mint
2 egg whites, beaten lightly
1 teaspoon finely chopped fresh mint, extra

Discard watermelon rind; blend or process watermelon until smooth. Push watermelon through sieve into large bowl; discard pulp. You need 2 1/2 cups watermelon juice for this recipe.

Combine sugar, the water and mint in medium pan; stir over heat, without boiling, until sugar dissolves. Simmer, uncovered, without stirring, about 10 minutes or until syrup is thick. Push syrup through sieve into large heatproof bowl; cool.

Stir watermelon juice into cooled syrup; pour into 8" x 12" pan. Cover with foil; freeze until just set. Blend or process watermelon ice with egg white until smooth, stir in extra mint, pour into 5" x 9" loaf pan. Cover, freeze overnight. *[Can be frozen up to 2 days.]*

Serve scoops of watermelon mint ice in glasses, with extra mint, if desired.

SERVES 4

Per serving 0.5g fat; 1.6g fiber; 168 cal (excluding extra mint).

Snacks

When you are absolutely ravenous between meals, it is very tempting to eat junk food. To help you resist, here is a great collection of delicious snacks that will pick you up without weighing you down. Some can be ready in minutes; others can be prepared ahead for those times when you know temptation is most likely to strike!

Roasted squash and cumin dip

1¹/₄ lb butternut squash, chopped coarsely
3 tablespoons cumin seed
2 cloves garlic, crushed
1¹/₂ tablespoons balsamic vinegar

Boil, steam or microwave squash until just tender; drain.

Combine squash with cumin and garlic in baking dish; bake, uncovered, at 500°F about 15 minutes or until squash is browned lightly. Lightly mash squash mixture with vinegar.

SERVES 4

Per serving 1.9g fat; 4.3g fiber; 114 cal.

Hummus

1¹/₂ tablespoons lemon juice
¹/₂ small yellow onion, chopped finely
1 clove garlic, crushed
¹/₂ teaspoon ground cumin
1 cup canned garbanzo beans, rinsed, drained
¹/₄ cup low-fat milk
1 teaspoon smooth peanut butter
¹/₄ teaspoon sesame oil
2 teaspoons chopped fresh cilantro

Heat lemon juice in small pan; add onion and garlic. Cook, stirring, until onion softens. Blend or process onion mixture with remaining ingredients until smooth.

SERVES 4

Per serving 3g fat; 5g fiber; 113 cal.

Quick beet dip

8 oz can sliced beets, drained
¹/₄ cup low-fat plain yogurt
1 teaspoon ground coriander
2 teaspoons ground cumin

Blend or process all ingredients until smooth.

SERVES 4

Per serving 0.8g fat; 1.5g fiber; 32 cal.

Bagel chips

Use plain, whole wheat, soy-and-linseed or any savory bagel of your choice.

2 savory bagels
cooking-oil spray
1 clove garlic, halved
3 tablespoons tandoori paste
3 tablespoons cream-style horseradish

Cut bagels into paper-thin rounds; place rounds, in single layer, on baking sheets. Coat rounds with cooking-oil spray; rub cut edge of garlic over rounds. Using pastry brush, spread half of the rounds with tandoori paste, then spread remaining rounds with horseradish. Bake, uncovered, at 350°F about 10 minutes or until browned lightly and crisp.

SERVES 4

Per serving 4.7g fat; 1.9g fiber; 178 cal.

Roasted squash and cumin dip *(center)*
Hummus *(right)*
Quick beet dip *(back)*
Bagel chips *(front)*

Corn bread with roast beef, arugula and horseradish

4 thick slices corn bread
1/4 cup low-fat sour cream
2 teaspoons cream-style horseradish
7 oz finely sliced rare roast beef
2 oz baby arugula leaves

Cut each slice of bread into 4 pieces. Combine sour cream and horseradish in small bowl; mix well. Top bread with roast beef and arugula; drizzle with horseradish cream.

SERVES 4

Per serving 14.4g fat; 4.2g fiber; 284 cal.

Spinach and feta focaccia

3 tablespoons lemon juice
1 medium yellow onion, sliced thinly
2 cloves garlic, crushed
4 oz baby spinach leaves
2 small focaccia
1 hard-boiled egg, grated finely
2 oz low-fat feta, crumbled

Heat juice in medium pan; cook onion and garlic, stirring, until onion softens. Stir in spinach; cook, stirring, until spinach is just wilted.

Cut a 2-inch-wide x 1 1/2-inch-deep wedge from top of each focaccia. Trim bread from under lids; reserve lids.

Place focaccia on baking sheet; fill with spinach mixture, pressing in firmly. Sprinkle egg and feta over spinach; replace lids. Bake, uncovered, at 450°F about 10 minutes or until bread is crisp. Cut into thick slices; serve with lemon wedges, if desired.

SERVES 4

Per serving 4.4g fat; 3.9g fiber; 286 cal (excluding lemon wedges).

Lamb focaccia

2 small yellow onions, chopped finely
2 cloves garlic, crushed
8 oz ground lamb
1 1/2 tablespoons tomato paste
1/4 teaspoon hot paprika
1 teaspoon ground cumin
2 small focaccia
1/4 cup finely grated low-fat mozzarella cheese
3 tablespoons finely chopped fresh mint

Heat oiled medium pan; cook onion and garlic, stirring, until onion softens. Add lamb, tomato paste, paprika and cumin; cook, stirring, until lamb is cooked through.

Split bread, place bottom halves on baking sheet, spread with lamb mixture, sprinkle with cheese and mint; replace tops. Bake, uncovered, at 450°F about 10 minutes or until bread is crisp. Cut into thick slices; serve with lemon wedges, if desired.

SERVES 4

Per serving 8.6g fat; 3.9g fiber; 370 cal (excluding lemon wedges).

Oven-dried corn tortilla chips

Can be prepared ahead.

8 corn tortillas
cooking-oil spray
2 teaspoons Cajun seasoning

Coat one side of one tortilla with cooking-oil spray, sprinkle with seasoning, cut into quarters. Place on baking sheet in single layer; bake, uncovered, at 325°F about 15 minutes or until crisp. If desired, place tortilla quarters over the handle of a wooden spoon to shape. Repeat with remaining tortillas, spray and seasoning. *[Can be made 2 days ahead; keep in an airtight container.]*

SERVES 4

Per serving 6.9g fat; 2.2g fiber; 188 cal.

Corn bread with roast beef, arugula and horseradish *(above left)*
Spinach and feta focaccia *(left)*
Lamb focaccia *(far left)*

Herb and garlic toasts

1 baguette loaf
cooking-oil spray
1 clove garlic, halved
1/4 cup finely chopped fresh parsley
1/4 cup finely chopped fresh chives
1/4 cup finely chopped fresh basil

Cut bread into 1-inch-wide diagonal slices; place, in single layer, on baking sheet. Coat tops with cooking-oil spray, rub with cut surface of garlic; sprinkle with combined herbs. Bake, uncovered, at 350°F about 7 minutes or until browned lightly.

SERVES 4
Per serving 3.3g fat; 2.3g fiber; 166 cal.

Spicy tomato dip

14 1/2 oz can tomatoes
2 cloves garlic, crushed
1 small yellow onion, sliced thinly
1 teaspoon Cajun seasoning

Combine undrained crushed tomatoes with remaining ingredients in small pan; cook, stirring, until onion is soft and sauce has thickened.

SERVES 4
Per serving 0.4g fat; 2g fiber; 28 cal.

Mediterranean ciabatta

3 medium sweet red bell peppers
4 small zucchini, sliced thinly lengthwise
2 large tomatoes, sliced thickly
cooking-oil spray
4 x 1-inch-thick slices ciabatta
1/4 cup baba ghanoush
1 1/2 tablespoons sun-dried tomato pesto
1 1/2 tablespoons fresh basil

Quarter bell peppers, remove and discard seeds and membranes. Roast under broiler or in oven at 500°F, skin-side up, until skin blisters and blackens. Cover bell peppers pieces in plastic or paper for 5 minutes, peel away skin.

Lightly coat zucchini and tomato with cooking-oil spray; cook, in batches, on heated grill plate (or broiler or barbecue) until browned both sides and just tender.

Toast ciabatta both sides; top with baba ghanoush, pesto, tomato, bell pepper, zucchini and basil.

SERVES 4
Per serving 2.8g fat; 5.1g fiber; 189 cal.

Baba ghanoush

Can be prepared ahead.

2 small eggplants, peeled, chopped coarsely
1/3 cup low-fat plain yogurt
1 1/2 tablespoons lemon juice
2 cloves garlic, crushed
1 teaspoon peanut butter
1 teaspoon ground cumin
1/2 teaspoon sesame oil
3 tablespoons finely chopped fresh cilantro

Place eggplant, in a single layer, in baking dish. Bake at 400°F about 40 minutes or until tender.

Blend or process eggplant with remaining ingredients until smooth. Cover; refrigerate about 30 minutes or until cool. *[Can be made a day ahead. Cover; refrigerate overnight.]*

SERVES 4
Per serving 2.3g fat; 3.2g fiber; 51 cal.

Oven-dried corn tortilla crisps *(below right)*
Herb and garlic toasts *(below left)*
Spicy tomato dip *(below center)*
Mediterranean ciabatta *(below back)*
Baba ghanoush *(below front)*

Potato wedges with two sauces (left)
Baked lemon-thyme ricotta with sourdough (back right)
Polenta triangles with smoked salmon (front right)

Potato wedges with two sauces

6 large potatoes
2 egg whites, beaten lightly
3 tablespoons garlic salt

SWEET CHILE DIPPING SAUCE
1/2 small sweet red bell pepper
3 small chiles, seeded, chopped finely
1/2 cup water
2 cloves garlic, crushed
1 cup sugar
2 teaspoons balsamic vinegar

LIME GUACAMOLE
1 small avocado, chopped coarsely
1/2 teaspoon finely grated lime rind
11/2 tablespoons lime juice
1 small red onion, chopped finely
1 medium tomato, seeded, chopped finely

Boil, steam or microwave unpeeled potatoes until just tender; drain. Cut potatoes into wedges; combine in large bowl with egg white and garlic salt. Place potato, in single layer, on oiled baking sheets; bake, uncovered, at 500°F about 30 minutes or until lightly browned and crisp. Serve with Sweet chile dipping sauce and Lime guacamole.

Sweet chile dipping sauce Halve bell pepper, remove and discard seeds and membranes. Roast under broiler or in oven at 500°F, skin-side up, until skin blisters and blackens. Cover bell pepper pieces in plastic or paper for 5 minutes, peel away skin; chop bell capsicum coarsely.

Blend or process bell pepper with chile, water and garlic until smooth. Combine bell pepper mixture with sugar and vinegar in medium pan; cook, stirring, until sugar dissolves. Simmer, uncovered, about 25 minutes or until sauce is thick and syrupy. *[Can be made 1 week ahead; store in refrigerator.]*

Lime guacamole Combine all ingredients in medium bowl; mix well.

SERVES 4
Per serving 9.2g fat; 10.5g fiber; 620 cal.

Baked lemon-thyme ricotta with sourdough

Baked lemon-thyme ricotta has to be made ahead. For best results, make the day before required. We used whole wheat sourdough, but any French bread could be used instead.

1 cup low-fat ricotta cheese
11/4 cups low-fat cottage cheese
1 egg, beaten lightly
1 clove garlic, crushed
11/2 tablespoons finely chopped fresh lemon thyme
3 tablespoons coarsely chopped pitted black olives
8 thin slices sourdough

Whisk ricotta in small bowl until smooth. Stir in cottage cheese, egg, garlic and half of the lemon thyme. Spoon mixture into oiled 2-cup ovenproof dish, sprinkle with olives. Bake, covered, at 350°F 35 minutes. Uncover, bake further 20 minutes or until just set. Sprinkle with remaining lemon thyme; cool.

Cover, refrigerate several hours until firm; drain off excess liquid. *[Should be made a day ahead.]*
Just before serving, toast bread, cut diagonally, serve with baked ricotta.

SERVES 4
Per serving 6.6g fat; 1.3g fiber; 221 cal.

Polenta triangles with smoked salmon

Can be partially prepared ahead. The polenta mixture needs to be refrigerated at least 1 hour before cutting into triangles and cooking.

2 cloves garlic, crushed
1 large yellow onion, chopped finely
4 medium potatoes
2 cups chicken stock
1/2 cup polenta
4 oz sliced smoked salmon
2 teaspoons finely grated lime rind
6 oz goat milk yogurt
2 teaspoons finely chopped fresh dill

Heat oiled small pan; cook garlic and onion, stirring, until onion softens.
Boil, steam or microwave potatoes until just tender; drain. Mash potatoes.
Bring stock to boil in medium pan, gradually add polenta; simmer, stirring, about 10 minutes or until soft and thick. Stir in onion mixture and potato. Spread mixture into oiled 6-inch-square cake pan; cool. Cover polenta; refrigerate until firm. *[Can be made a day ahead.]*
Remove polenta from pan; cut polenta in half to form two 3-inch x 6-inch rectangles. Cut each rectangle to give six 1-inch-wide x 3-inch-long x 2-inch-deep fingers. Turn fingers so 2-inch side is facing; cut in half diagonally to form 2 triangles (24 triangles in all).
Heat oiled large pan; cook polenta triangles, in batches, until golden brown all over and heated through. Cut salmon to fit triangles. Top polenta triangles with salmon and combined rind, yogurt and dill.

MAKES 24
Per triangle 0.6g fat; 0.8g fiber; 48 cal.

Beef empanadas

Can be partially prepared ahead. We used canned pinto beans with chili sauce for this recipe.

1³/₄ cups all-purpose flour
2 oz low-fat quark cheese
¹/₂ cup warm water, approximately
8 oz ground beef
1 teaspoon ground cumin
¹/₂ x 15 oz can Mexican-style chili beans
1¹/₂ tablespoons finely chopped fresh oregano

Blend or process flour and cheese until combined; add enough water to make a soft, sticky dough. Turn dough onto floured surface; knead until smooth. Wrap in plastic wrap; let stand 30 minutes. *[Can be made 1 day ahead; refrigerate until required.]*

Meanwhile, for filling, cook beef and cumin in heated medium pan until browned. Add beans; cook until mixture is heated through. Stir in oregano; cool.

Roll out dough on floured surface until ¹/₈-inch thick. Cut 4-inch rounds from pastry and re-rolled scraps. You will get approximately 24 rounds.

Place 1 rounded tablespoon of filling in center of each round, fold round in half to enclose filling; pinch edges to seal. Cover tightly with plastic wrap; refrigerate 15 minutes. *[Can be made up to 3 hours ahead.]*

Place empanadas on parchment-paper-lined baking sheets; bake, uncovered, at 400°F about 15 minutes or until brown and crisp.

SERVES 4

Per serving 8.2g fat; 4.5g fiber; 364 cal.

Bread samosas

Can be partially prepared ahead.

1 large potato, chopped finely
5 green onions, sliced thinly
1¹/₂ tablespoons mild curry powder
10¹/₂ oz can garbanzo beans, rinsed, drained
¹/₂ cup frozen peas, thawed
1¹/₂ tablespoons tomato paste
¹/₄ cup water
24 slices white bread
cooking-oil spray

Heat oiled medium pan, cook potato and onion, stirring, until onion is soft. Add curry powder, cook, stirring, until fragrant. Add garbanzos, peas, tomato paste and water, cook, uncovered, until potato is tender, stirring occasionally; cool. *[Can be made 1 day ahead; cover, refrigerate until required.]*

Cut bread into 4-inch rounds. Place a rounded tablespoon of potato mixture on each round, brush edges with a little water, fold rounds in half to enclose filling; press edges together with a fork. Place samosas on greased baking sheets; coat with cooking-oil spray. Bake, uncovered, at 350°F about 20 minutes or until brown and crisp.

MAKES 24

Per samosa 0.8g fat; 1.3g fiber; 59 cal.

Tandoori chicken bites

Soak bamboo skewers in water for at least 1 hour before using to prevent them burning.

1 lb boneless, skinless chicken breast halves
3 tablespoons tandoori paste
1 cup low-fat plain yogurt
1 teaspoon ground cumin
1 teaspoon ground coriander
1 burpless cucumber, peeled, seeded, chopped finely
1¹/₂ tablespoons lemon juice
1¹/₂ tablespoons finely chopped fresh cilantro

Cut chicken into bite-size pieces; combine with tandoori paste, ¹/₂ cup of the yogurt, half the cumin and half the ground coriander in medium bowl. Cover; refrigerate 3 hours or overnight.

Thread chicken onto skewers; cook, in batches, on heated oiled grill pan (or broiler or barbecue) until browned all over and cooked through.

Meanwhile, combine remaining yogurt with remaining cumin and ground coriander, cucumber, juice and fresh cilantro in small bowl; mix well.

Serve Tandoori chicken bites with yogurt mixture.

SERVES 8

Per serving 2.1g fat; 0.4g fiber; 100 cal.

Beef empanadas *(back left)*
Bread samosas *(center left)*
Tandoori chicken bites *(front left)*
Chile shrimp and mango cups *(above right)*
Vegetable rolls with dipping sauce *(right)*

Chile shrimp and mango cups

3 sheets filo pastry
cooking-oil spray
7 oz shelled small cooked shrimp,
**   chopped finely**
1 small mango, chopped finely
1/2 small red onion, chopped finely
1 small chile, seeded, chopped finely
3 tablespoons finely chopped
**   fresh chives**

Cut filo into 2-inch squares. Layer
4 squares together, spraying with oil
between each layer and ensuring corners
do not cover those of previous square,
to make 1 stack. Repeat with remaining
squares to make 52 stacks.

Press 12 stacks into oiled 12-hole
small (3 tablespoon) muffin pan. Bake at
350°F 5 minutes or until browned.
Repeat with remaining stacks.

Combine shrimp, mango, onion,
chile and chives in small bowl; spoon
rounded teaspoons of mixture into
pastry cases.

MAKES 52
Per cup 0.3g fat; 0.1g fiber; 11 cal.

Vegetable rolls with dipping sauce

1 large carrot
2 burpless cucumbers, peeled, seeded
2 medium sweet red bell peppers,
**   seeded**
1/3 cup lime juice
3 tablespoons chopped fresh cilantro
12 x 8-inch-round rice paper sheets
1/2 cup firmly packed brown sugar
1/4 cup water
1/4 cup mild sweet chili sauce

Cut carrot, cucumber and bell pepper
into thin 2-inch-long strips; combine
with 1 1/2 tablespoons of the lime juice
and 2 teaspoons of the coriander in
medium bowl, divide into 12 portions.

Place 1 sheet rice paper in large
heatproof bowl of hot water, soak about
1 minute or until softened; gently lift
from water, place on board. Place
1 portion vegetable mixture across lower
edge of rice paper; fold in sides, roll to
enclose filling. Repeat with remaining
rice paper sheets and vegetable mixture.

Place remaining juice, sugar, water
and sauce in small pan; stir over heat,
without boiling, until sugar is dissolved.
Simmer, uncovered, without stirring,
about 5 minutes or until mixture thickens;
cool. Stir in remaining cilantro; serve.

SERVES 4
Per serving 0.8g fat; 4.4g fiber; 215 cal.

Breakfast and drinks

If you are bored with the same old toast-and-grapefruit breakfast, get your day off to a new start with something a little different. From yummy dishes you can whip up in a trice for a leisurely weekend brunch, to refreshing fruit drinks you can sip as you head for the door, all the recipes in this chapter combine delicious flavors with a fresh, low-fat approach.

Eggs with asparagus, grilled ham and onion jam

We used medium eggs for this recipe.

2 medium red onions, sliced thinly
3 tablespoons balsamic vinegar
1/3 cup firmly packed brown sugar
3 tablespoons chicken stock
4 oz thinly sliced ham
1 lb asparagus, trimmed
4 eggs

Heat medium oiled pan; cook onion, stirring, until almost soft. Stir in vinegar and sugar; cook, stirring, until sugar dissolves. Stir in stock; simmer, uncovered, about 15 minutes or until onion caramelizes, cool.

Place ham, in single layer, on baking sheet; broil until browned lightly.

Boil, steam or microwave asparagus until just tender; drain.

Heat oiled large pan; fry eggs until cooked as desired. Serve eggs with asparagus, ham and onion jam.

SERVES 4

Per serving 6.3g fat; 2.6g fiber; 207 cal.

Swiss muesli with grilled mangoes and blueberries

11/2 cups old-fashioned rolled oats
1 cup low-fat milk
10 oz low-fat yogurt with honey
2 medium mangoes
1 medium apple, chopped finely
3 tablespoons lemon juice
4 oz fresh blueberries
3 tablespoons honey

Combine oats, half the milk and half the yogurt in large bowl; cover, refrigerate 20 minutes.

Meanwhile, cut through mangoes on both sides of seed; scoop out flesh with a spoon. Cut mango halves into thick slices. Cook mango on heated grill pan (or broiler or barbecue) until browned both sides.

Stir remaining milk, remaining yogurt, apple and juice into oat mixture. Top with blueberries and grilled mango, drizzle with honey.

SERVES 4

Per serving 4.3g fat; 5.7g fiber; 366 cal.

Gazpacho juice

31/2 cups tomato juice
1 small red onion, chopped
1 small cucumber, peeled, chopped
1 small chile, seeded, chopped
11/2 tablespoons Worcestershire sauce
1/4 cup lime juice
4 untrimmed celery stalks

Blend or process tomato juice, onion, cucumber, chile, sauce and lime juice until smooth. Divide between four glasses; garnish with celery.

SERVES 4

Per serve 0.2g fat; 2.7g fiber; 68 cal.

Eggs with asparagus, grilled ham and onion jam *(far right)*
Swiss muesli with grilled mangoes and blueberries *(back)*
Gazpacho juice *(front)*

Pancakes with spiced bananas

1 cup sugar
10 cloves
3 tablespoons dark rum
$^1/_2$ cup water
1 cup self-rising flour
1 cup buttermilk
2 egg whites
2 large bananas, sliced diagonally

Combine sugar, cloves, rum and water in small pan; stir over heat, without boiling, until sugar dissolves. Bring to boil; simmer, uncovered, about 5 minutes or until syrup is slightly thickened.

Meanwhile, combine flour, milk and egg whites in large bowl; whisk until batter is smooth. Heat oiled large pan. Pour in 3 tablespoons batter for each pancake; cook until browned lightly both sides. Repeat with remaining batter.

Place bananas, in single layer, on oiled baking sheet, brush with 3 tablespoons syrup; reserve remaining syrup. Broil bananas until just soft and browned.

For each serving, place 1 pancake on serving plate, top with $^1/_8$ of the banana mixture, another pancake, another $^1/_8$ of the banana mixture, then another pancake. Drizzle with reserved syrup.

SERVES 4

Per serving 1.8g fat; 3.1g fiber; 510 cal.

Porridge with sticky fruits

1 cup dried apricots
3 tablespoons honey
1 cup water
1 cinnamon stick
$1^1/_2$ tablespoons finely grated lemon rind
1 cup fresh dates
$2^1/_4$ cups old-fashioned rolled oats
6 cups low-fat milk
$1^1/_2$ tablespoons sliced almonds, toasted

Combine apricots, honey, water, cinnamon and rind in small pan; bring to boil. Simmer, uncovered, about 5 minutes or until syrup has thickened slightly; cool. Cut dates in half lengthwise, discard pits; add dates to apricot mixture.

Combine oats and milk in medium pan; cook, stirring, about 10 minutes or until mixture thickens.

Drain fruit over large bowl; reserve syrup. Spoon porridge into bowls; top with apricots, dates and nuts, drizzle with syrup.

SERVES 4

Per serving 5.6g fat; 21.5g fiber; 597 cal.

Mango buttermilk booster

1 large mango, chopped coarsely
1 cup buttermilk
1 cup low-fat milk
3 tablespoons low-fat powdered milk
4 ice-cubes
1 scoop low-fat ice cream

Blend or process all ingredients until smooth.

SERVES 2
Per serving 4.8g fat; 3.2g fiber; 346 cal.

Fruit cup crush

2 large mangoes
1/2 medium cantaloupe
1 medium pineapple
2 cups orange juice
3 tablespoons superfine sugar

Cut peeled fruit into medium pieces. Blend or process fruit, in batches, until smooth. Stir in orange juice and sugar.

SERVES 4 (Makes about 6 cups)
Per serving 1.4g fat; 12.4g fiber; 402 cal.

Mixed fruit and yogurt drink

You will need about 3 passion fruit for this recipe.

1/2 small papaya
1 large orange
2 medium kiwi fruit
1/2 small pineapple
1/2 cup blueberries
5 oz raspberries
1/4 cup fresh passion fruit pulp
1/2 cup low-fat plain yogurt

Peel papaya, orange, kiwi fruit and pineapple; cut fruit into medium pieces. Blend or process fruit and remaining ingredients, in batches, until smooth.

SERVES 8 (Makes about 8 cups)
Per serving 0.8g fat; 4.5g fiber; 63 cal.

Fruit cup crush; mixed fruit and yogurt drink; mango buttermilk booster *(front to back)*

Pancakes with spiced bananas *(top left)*
Porridge with sticky fruits *(far left)*

French fruit toast with maple yogurt

1 egg white
1/2 cup low-fat milk
6 slices fruit loaf
7 oz low-fat vanilla yogurt
1 1/2 tablespoons maple syrup

Whisk egg white and milk in large bowl until combined. Cut bread in half diagonally. Heat oiled large pan; dip each piece of bread into milk mixture. Cook, in batches, until browned lightly both sides. To serve, place 3 pieces of toast on each plate, top with combined yogurt and syrup. Serve with fresh berries, if desired.

SERVES 4

Per serving 2g fat; 1.3g fiber; 184 cal (excluding berries).

Ham, avocado and roasted tomato toast

4 large plum tomatoes
1 1/2 tablespoons brown sugar
1 small red onion, sliced thinly
5 oz thinly sliced ham
4 thick slices vienna loaf
1/2 small avocado, sliced thinly
1 1/2 tablespoons shredded fresh basil

Cut tomatoes in half lengthwise; place cut-side up on oiled baking sheet, sprinkle with sugar. Bake tomato, uncovered, at 500°F 15 minutes. Add onion; bake further 15 minutes or until tomato is soft.

Cook ham in heated small pan until browned lightly and almost crisp. Toast bread; top with ham, onion, tomato, avocado and basil.

SERVES 4

Per serving 5.9g fat; 2.6g fiber; 156 cal.

French fruit toast with maple yogurt *(above left)*
Ham, avocado and roasted tomato toast *(left)*
Low-fat toasted muesli *(above right)*
Bagels with scrambled eggs and smoked salmon *(above right, center)*
Quick banana bread *(above far right)*

Low-fat toasted muesli

We used All-Bran cereal.

2 cups old-fashioned rolled oats
1/2 cup bran cereal
1/2 cup honey
1/2 cup fresh orange juice
1/2 cup coarsely chopped
  dried apricots
1/2 cup coarsely chopped
  dried apples
1/2 cup raisins
1/4 cup dried currants
3 cups puffed rice

Combine oats and bran in large bowl.
  Heat honey and orange juice in small
pan, stirring until honey is melted.
Add half of the honey mixture to oat
mixture; mix well. Spread mixture over
parchment-paper-lined baking sheet;
bake, uncovered, at 325°F about
20 minutes or until browned lightly,
stirring every 5 minutes.
  Return mixture to same large
bowl, add remaining ingredients and
remaining honey mixture; spread over
2 parchment-paper-lined baking sheets.
Bake, uncovered, at 325°F about
10 minutes or until browned lightly,

stirring midway through cooking time;
cool. Store in an airtight container up
to 2 weeks.

MAKES 8 CUPS

Per cup 2.6g fat; 4.6g fiber; 261 cal.

Bagels with scrambled eggs and smoked salmon

2 eggs, beaten lightly
10 egg whites
3 tablespoons finely chopped
  fresh chives
2 bagels
1 small cucumber, sliced thinly
7 oz sliced smoked salmon

Whisk eggs, whites and chives
together in medium bowl. Heat
oiled medium pan, add egg mixture,
gently stir over low heat until
almost set.
  Split bagels in half; toast both
sides. Top bagel halves with cucumber,
eggs and salmon.

SERVES 4

Per serving 7g fat; 2.1g fiber; 291 cal.

Quick banana bread

You will need 1 large overripe banana
for this recipe.

1 1/4 cups self-rising flour
1 teaspoon ground cinnamon
1 1/2 tablespoons low-fat margarine
1/2 cup sugar
1 egg, beaten lightly
1/4 cup low-fat milk
1/2 cup mashed banana

Line base and sides of 5" x 9"
loaf pan with parchment paper.
  Combine flour and cinnamon in
large bowl; rub in margarine. Stir in
sugar, egg, milk and banana; do not
overmix, batter should be lumpy.
Spoon mixture into prepared pan;
bake at 450°F about 20 minutes
or until cooked when tested.

SERVES 4

Per serving 4g fat; 2.8g fiber; 332 cal.

GLOSSARY

Image labels (clockwise): ricotta, cottage cheese, quark, goat cheese, feta, parmesan, mozzarella, cheddar

ALCOHOL AND LIQUEURS
Cointreau an orange-flavored liqueur.
Frangelico a hazelnut-flavored liqueur.
Grand Marnier an orange-flavored liqueur.
Rum, dark we prefer to use an underproof rum.
Tia Maria a coffee-flavored liqueur.

ANGOSTURA AROMATIC BITTERS
Angostura is a brand of bitters, based on rum, infused with aromatic bark, herbs and spices.

ASIAN PEAR
Also called Japanese or nashi pear; similar in appearance to an apple.

BABA GHANOUSH
Dip based on eggplant, tahini, garlic and salt.

BAGEL
Small, ring-shaped bread roll, boiled in water then baked.

BEAN SPROUTS
Also known as bean shoots. New growths of beans and seeds, such as mung bean, soy bean, alfalfa and snow pea sprouts.

BEEF AND VEAL
Beef eye fillet tenderloin.
Beef rump steak boneless tender cut.
Veal leg steaks best cut to have pounded into schnitzels or scaloppine.
Veal rib chops choice cut from the mid-loin (back) area.

BREADCRUMBS
Fresh 1- or 2-day-old bread made into crumbs by blending or processing.
Packaged fine-textured, purchased white breadcrumbs.

BURPLESS CUCUMBER
Long and thin-skinned. Also known as the European or Lebanese cucumber.

CAJUN SEASONING
This packaged mix of herbs and spices can include paprika, basil, onion, fennel, thyme, cayenne and white pepper.

CANTELOUPE
Also known as rockmelon.

CAPERS
The grey-green buds of a warm-climate shrub. The buds are sold pickled, or dried and salted. Their piquancy adds to dressings and sauces.

CARAWAY
Available in seed or ground form; used in sweet and savory dishes.

CARDAMOM
Can be bought in pod, seed or ground form. Has a distinctive, aromatic, sweetly rich flavor.

CHEESE
Cheddar cheese, low-fat we used one with a fat content of not more than 7%.
Cottage cheese we used one with 2g fat per 4 oz.
Feta cheese, low-fat we used a feta with an average fat content of 15%.
Goat cheese made from goat milk. Has an earthy, strong taste and is available in both soft and firm textures.
Mozzarella, low-fat we used one with 17.5g fat per 4 oz.
Parmesan a sharp-tasting, dry, hard cheese, made from skim or part-skim milk and aged for at least a year.
Quark a soft, mildly sour cheese made from skim milk with 9.5g fat per 4 oz.
Ricotta, low-fat a fresh, unripened cheese made from whey with 8.5g fat per 4 oz.

CHICKEN TENDERLOIN
Thin strip of meat under the breast.

CHILI POWDER
Made from ground chiles, it can be used as a substitute for fresh chiles in the proportion of $1/2$ teaspoon ground chili powder to 1 medium chopped fresh chile.

CHILES
Also known as hot peppers; available in many types and sizes. Generally, the smaller the chile the hotter it is. Use rubber gloves when seeding and chopping fresh chiles as they can burn your skin. Removing membranes and seeds reduces the heat level.

CHINESE CABBAGE
Also known as Peking cabbage or wong bok.

CHOY SUM
Also known as flowering bok choy or flowering white cabbage.

CIABATTA
Italian crusty wood-fired bread.

CILANTRO
Also known as fresh coriander or Chinese parsley. Bright-green-leafed herb with a pungent flavor.

COOKING-OIL SPRAY
We used a cholesterol-free non-stick cooking spray made from canola oil.

CORNSTARCH
Also known as cornflour; used as a thickening agent in cooking.

CORN SYRUP
Available in light or dark color; either can be substituted for the other. Glucose syrup (liquid glucose) can be substituted.

COUSCOUS
A fine grain-like cereal product, made from semolina.

CRACKER BREAD
Flat sheets of unleavened bread, also known as lavosh.

CREAM
Half-and-half (10.5–18% butterfat) a mixture of milk and cream that, like light cream, is sometimes substituted for heavy or whipping cream when lighter, less rich results are desired. Neither half-and-half nor light cream holds its shape when whipped.
Low-fat sour cream we used light sour cream with 5g fat per $1/4$ cup.
Low-fat thickened cream also known as light whipping cream. We used thickened cream with 11g fat per $1/4$ cup.

EGGPLANT
Also known as aubergine.

EXTRACTS
Also known as essences; generally the byproduct of distillation of plants.

FILO PASTRY
Also known as phyllo. Chilled or frozen purchased tissue-thin pastry sheets that are very versatile, lending themselves to both sweet and savory dishes.

FISH FILLETS
Fish pieces that have been boned and skinned.

FLOUR
All-purpose plain flour.
Self-rising all-purpose flour sifted with baking powder (a raising agent consisting mainly of 2 parts cream of tartar to 1 part bicarbonate of soda) in the proportion of 1 cup flour to 2 level teaspoons baking powder.

FRENCH DRESSING Use any oil-free or fat-free variety.

GARBANZO BEANS Round sandy-coloured legumes, also known as chickpeas, hummus or channa.

GELATIN We used powdered gelatin.

GHEE Clarified butter; with the milk solids removed, this fat can be heated to high temperature without burning.

GINGER, FRESH also known as green or root ginger. The thick, gnarled root of a tropical plant.

GOAT MILK YOGURT Available from health food stores.

GREEN PEPPERCORNS Unripe berry of the pepper plant usually sold packed in brine.

HAZELNUTS Also known as filberts. Rich, sweet nut with a brown inedible skin that is removed by rubbing heated nuts in a tea towel.

HERBS We have specified when to use fresh and dried herbs. We used dried (not ground) herbs in the ratio of 1:4 for fresh herbs.

HORSERADISH
Cream-style a creamy prepared paste of grated horseradish, vinegar, oil and sugar.
Fresh a plant of the mustard family; the root has a hot, pungent flavor and is often used as a condiment.

ITALIAN DRESSING Use an oil-free or fat-free variety.

KAFFIR LIME
Fruit medium-sized citrus fruit with wrinkly yellow-green skin, used in Thai cooking.
Leaves aromatic leaves used fresh or dried in Asian dishes.

KETJAP MANIS Indonesian sweet, thick soy sauce which has sugar and spices added.

KIWI FRUIT Also known as Chinese gooseberry.

LAMB
Eye of loin a cut from a row of loin chops, with the bone and fat removed.
Tenderloin small piece of meat from row of loin chops or cutlets.

LEMON GRASS A sharp-edged grass, smelling and tasting of lemon. The white lower part of each stem is used.

LEMON PEPPER SEASONING A blend of crushed black peppercorns, lemon, herbs and spices.

LENTILS Many varieties of dried legumes, identified by and named after their color.

LOW-FAT ICE CREAM We used an ice-cream with 3% fat.

LOW-FAT MARGARINE We used polyunsaturated spread, containing 2g of fat per 5g.

LOW-FAT MAYONNAISE We used cholesterol-free mayonnaise with 3g fat per 4 oz.

LOW-FAT YOGURT We used yogurt with a fat content of less than 0.2%.

MAPLE-FLAVORED SYRUP Also known as pancake syrup. Made from cane sugar and artificial maple flavoring; is not the same as maple syrup.

MAPLE SYRUP Distilled sap of the maple tree.

MEXICAN CHILI POWDER A blend of chili powder, cumin, oregano, garlic and salt.

MILK
Buttermilk cultured milk with 4.5g fat per cup and a slightly sour taste. Low-fat yogurt can be substituted.
Evaporated, low-fat we used canned milk with 4g fat per cup.
Low-fat we used low-fat milk with 3.5g fat per cup.
Skim we used skim milk with 0.25g fat per cup.

MIRIN A sweet low-alcohol rice wine used in Japanese cooking.

MIXED BABY LETTUCE LEAVES Often sold as mesclun; consists of an assortment of edible greens and flowers.

MIZUNA Feathery green salad leaf with a sharp flavor.

MUSHROOMS
Button small, cultivated white mushrooms with a delicate, subtle flavor.
Italian brown light to dark brown mushrooms with mild, earthy flavor.
Shiitake cultivated fresh mushroom; has a rich, meaty flavor.

MUSTARD
Black mustard seed also known as brown mustard seed. More pungent than the white (or yellow) seed used in most mustards.
Dijon a pale brown, fairly mild French mustard.
Stone-ground a flavorful coarse-grain mustard made from crushed mustard seed.

NAAN An Indian flat bread, slightly leavened with yeast.

NOODLES
Bean thread noodles also known as cellophane or glass noodles, or bean thread vermicelli.
Fresh egg noodles made from wheat flour and eggs; strands vary in thickness.
Ramen a crinkly or straight dried wheat noodle.
Soba a buckwheat noodle. Comes in varying proportions of buckwheat and wheat flour; the color varies accordingly, from brownish through to almost white.

OIL
Extra virgin olive oil the highest quality olive oil, obtained from the first pressing of the olives.
Olive mono-unsaturated. Made from the pressing of tree-ripened olives. Good for everyday cooking and as a salad-dressing ingredient.
Peanut pressed from ground peanuts. The most commonly used oil in stir-frying because of its high smoke point.

Fresh herbs

1. Lemon thyme
2. Sage
3. Marjoram
4. Rosemary
5. Curly parsley
6. Italian parsley
7. Cilantro
8. Dill
9. Tarragon
10. Thyme
11. Chives
12. Mint
13. Basil

canteloupe

papaya

Asian pear

kiwi fruit

Sesame made from roasted, crushed, white sesame seed; used as a flavoring.

Vegetable any of a number of oils having a plant rather than an animal source.

ONION
Green also known as scallion or (incorrectly) shallot. An immature onion picked before the bulb has formed, having a bright-green edible stalk.
Red also known as Spanish, red Spanish or Bermuda onion. A sweet flavored, large, purple-red onion; good eaten raw in salads.
Yellow and white are interchangeable. Their pungent flesh adds flavor to a vast range of dishes.

PANCETTA An Italian salt-cured pork roll, usually cut from the belly. Bacon can be substituted in most recipes.

PAPAYA Tropical fruit also known as pawpaw.

PAPRIKA Ground dried red bell pepper, available mild or hot.

PARSLEY, ITALIAN Also known as continental parsley or flat-leaf parsley.

PASSION FRUIT Also known as granadilla. A small tropical fruit, native to Brazil, with edible black seeds.

PASTA
Fettuccine ribbon pasta averaging 1/4 inch in width, made from durum wheat semolina and egg, available fresh or dried, plain or flavored with various herbs, pepper or vegetable essences.
Gnocchi Italian "dumplings"

made of potatoes, semolina or flour; cooked in boiling water or baked with a sauce.
Lasagna available as fresh or dried, instant sheets.
Spinach and ricotta tortellini small rounds of pasta, filled with spinach and ricotta, then sealed.

PECANS Golden-brown, buttery, rich nuts. Good in savory and sweet dishes.

PINE NUTS Also known as pignoli; small, cream-colored kernels from the cones of various pine trees.

PIZZA SAUCE We used a ready-made pizza sauce consisting of tomatoes, herbs and spices.

POCKET PITA Lebanese wheat-flour bread that can be split to form a pocket.

POLENTA A flour-like cereal made of ground corn; similar to cornmeal but coarser. Also the dish made from it.

POTATOES
Fingerling small and finger-shaped with a nutty flavor; good baked.
New potatoes also known as baby potatoes; can be any variety of potato, harvested when young enough to retain a waxy appearance and paper-thin skin.
Pink eye small with deep pink eyes; good steamed, boiled or baked.

SHRIMP Also known as prawns.

PROSCIUTTO Salted-cured, air-dried (unsmoked), pressed ham; usually sold in paper-thin slices, ready to eat.

PUMPKIN Sometimes used interchangeably with the word squash, the pumpkin is a member of the gourd family. Various types can be substituted for one another.

RAISINS Sweet dried grapes.

RED CURRANT JELLY
A preserve made from red currants; used as a glaze for desserts and meats, or in sauces.

RICE
Arborio small, round rice; especially good in risottos.
Brown natural whole grain.
Calrose a medium-grain, extremely versatile variety.
Paper mostly from Vietnam (banh trang). Made from rice paste and stamped into rounds. Dipped momentarily in water, they become pliable wrappers for fried food and fresh (uncooked) vegetables.

orange sweet potato

pink eye potato

new potato

fingerling potato

Puffed grains puffed under heat.
Wild from North America with a distinctive flavor; not a member of the rice family; difficult to cultivate.

ROLLED OATS, OLD-FASHIONED Whole oat grains that have been steamed and flattened. Not the quick-cook variety.

ROSEWATER EXTRACT Made from crushed rose petals; used for its aromatic quality in many desserts.

SAMBAL OELEK Also ulek or olek. A salty paste of ground chillies, sugar and spices.

SAUCES
Barbecue tomato-based sauce used to marinate and baste.
Black bean made from fermented soybeans, water and wheat flour.
Catsup made from tomatoes, vinegar and spices.
Fish also called nam pla or nuoc nam; made from salted, pulverised, fermented fish. Has a pungent smell and strong taste; use sparingly.
Hoisin a thick, sweet and spicy Chinese paste made from salted, fermented soybeans, onions and garlic; used as a marinade or baste, or to accent stir-fries and barbecued or roasted foods.
Oyster Asian in origin, this rich, brown sauce is made from oysters and their brine, cooked with salt and soy sauce; thickened with starch.

Plum a thick, sweet and sour sauce made from plums, vinegar, sugar, chiles and spices.
Soy made from fermented soybeans.
Sweet chili a comparatively mild, Thai-type sauce made from red chiles, sugar, garlic and vinegar.
Tabasco brand name of an extremely fiery sauce made from vinegar, hot red peppers and salt.
Teriyaki a sauce consisting of soy sauce, corn syrup, vinegar, ginger and other spices; a distinctive glaze on grilled meats.
Worcestershire a dark-brown spicy sauce used to season

meat, gravies and cocktails, and as a condiment.

SESAME SEED Black and white are the most common varieties of these oval seeds. To toast: spread seed evenly on oven tray, toast in 350°F oven briefly.

SNOW PEAS Also called mange tout ("eat all").

SOURDOUGH Crunchy, crusted bread with soft inner crumb, a distinctive aroma and a sour flavor.

STAR ANISE A dried star-shaped pod, the seed of which tastes of aniseed.

STOCK 1 cup stock is the equivalent of 1 cup water plus 1 crumbled bouillon cube or 1 teaspoon bouillon powder.

SUGAR We used coarse, granulated table sugar, also known as crystal sugar, unless otherwise specified.
Brown an extremely soft, fine granulated sugar retaining molasses for its deep colour and flavor.
Demerara raw granulated sugar, pale brown in color.
Palm sugar from the coconut palm; usually sold in compressed cakes. Also known as gula jawa, gula melaka and jaggery. Brown sugar can be substituted.
Powdered sugar also known as icing sugar mixture; granulated sugar crushed together with a small amount (about 3%) of cornstarch added.
Superfine also known as caster or finely granulated table sugar.

SUGAR SNAP PEAS Small pods with formed peas inside; eaten whole, raw or cooked.

SUN-DRIED TOMATOES Available loose (by weight) or in packets (not packed in oil).

TACO SEASONING packaged seasoning made from oregano, cumin, chiles and other spices.

TANDOORI PASTE Indian blend of spices, including turmeric, paprika, chili powder, saffron, cardamom and garam masala.

TAT SOI Also known as rosette pak choy, tai gu choy, Chinese flat cabbage; a variety of bok choy.

TEMPEH Flat cakes made from soy beans. Tofu may be used instead.

TIKKA MASALA Indian paste of chile, coriander, cumin, garlic, ginger, turmeric, oil, fennel, pepper, cinnamon and cardamom.

TOFU Also known as bean curd; an off-white, custard-like product made from the "milk" of crushed soybeans; comes fresh, as soft or firm, and processed, as fried or pressed dried sheets. Fresh tofu can be refrigerated in water (changed daily) up to 4 days.

TOMATOES
Paste triple-concentrated tomato puree used to flavor soups, stews and sauces.
Plum tomatoes also called egg or Roma; smallish, oval-shaped tomatoes.
Puree canned pureed tomatoes (not tomato paste). Substitute with fresh peeled and pureed tomatoes.

TORTILLA Round, unleavened bread, made from either corn or wheat flour.

VANILLA BEAN Dried, long, thin pod from an orchid. The minuscule black seeds inside the bean are used to impart a luscious vanilla flavor in baking and desserts.

VINEGAR
Balsamic vinegar authentic only from Italian province of Modena; made from a local wine of white Trebbiano grapes specially processed then aged in antique wooden casks to give the exquisite pungent flavor.
Brown malt vinegar made from fermented malt barley and beech shavings.
Cider vinegar made from fermented apples.
Raspberry vinegar made from fresh raspberries steeped in a white wine vinegar.
Red wine vinegar based on red wine.
Rice vinegar made from fermented rice. Also known as seasoned rice vinegar.
Sherry vinegar mellow wine vinegar named for its color.

White wine vinegar made from fermented white wine.

WATER CHESTNUTS Resemble chestnuts in appearance, hence the English name. Small brown tubers with a crisp, white nutty-tasting flesh. Their crunchy texture is best experienced fresh, however canned and frozen water chestnuts are more easily obtained and can be kept about a month, once opened, under refrigeration.

WATERCRESS Small, crisp, deep green, rounded leaves having a slightly bitter, peppery flavor. Good addition to salads, soups and as an ingredient in sandwiches.

WONTON WRAPPERS, FRESH Small raw pastry wrappers available from Asian supermarkets. Gow gee, egg or spring roll pastry sheets can be substituted.

YELLOW BABY SQUASH Also known as pattypan, summer squash or scallopine. Small yellow or green thin-skinned squash.

ZUCCHINI Also known as courgette.

sourdough

bagel

ciabatta

cracker bread

focaccia

pita pocket

INDEX

Apple and cinnamon cakes
with lemon syrup, *96*
Asian greens, Stir-fried, *76*
Asian pears, Grilled, with
rosewater syrup, *92*
asparagus, Grilled, prosciutto
and peach salad, *19*

Baba ghanoush, *101*
Bacon, buttermilk and chive
puree, *88*
Bagel chips, *98*
Bagels with scrambled eggs
and smoked salmon, *111*
Baked lemon-thyme ricotta
with sourdough, *102*
banana bread, Quick, *111*
Beans
Beans and sugar snap peas
with lemon and capers, *74*
Chili beans with spicy
tortilla crisps, *66*
fava bean medley, Zucchini,
squash and, *82*
Green bean and asparagus
salad with citrus dressing,
83
Orange hazelnut beans, *72*
White beans in rich tomato
sauce, *86*

Beef
Beef empanadas, *104*
Beef with red wine sauce
and polenta, *51*
Cajun beef roll, *24*
Moroccan beef salad with
couscous, *6*
Seasoned beef tenderloin,
71
Steaks with bell pepper
salsa, *46*
Stir-fried Mexican beef, *25*
Teriyaki beef skewers, *65*
Thai beef salad, *68*
beet dip, Quick, *98*
bell pepper, Roasted,
and olive salad, *76*
bell pepper, Roasted red,
tarts, *67*
bell pepper rolls,
Mediterranean-style, *30*
Black and white sesame
crusted lamb, *43*
Brandied carrots and leek, *79*
Bread samosas, *104*

Caesar-style salad, Low-fat, *81*
Cajun beef roll, *24*
Carrot and lentil soup with
caraway toast, *55*

carrots, Brandied, and leek, *79*
Char-grilled chicken with
mango salsa, *38*
Char-grilled octopus with
tomatoes and garbanzos, *65*
Chicken
Char-grilled chicken with
mango salsa, *38*
Chicken and mushroom
pastry packets, *61*
Chicken and pickled
cucumber pita, *22*
Chicken and tomato
omelette, *24*
Chicken chile stir-fry, *28*
Chicken, corn and noodle
chowder, *8*
Chicken, lentil and spinach
pasta, *48*
Chicken with red pesto
pasta, *41*
Citrus chicken with garbanzo
salad, *60*
Ginger, chicken and lime
patties, *41*
Herbed chicken kebabs with
toasted pecans, *60*
Light 'n' spicy crumbed
chicken, *43*
Poached chicken with
tropical salsa, *40*
Sesame chicken noodle
salad, *17*
Spicy chicken fried rice, *13*
Sweet soy chicken and
noodles, *27*
Tandoori chicken bites, *104*
Thai-style chicken and
vegetable curry, *32*
Chili beans with spicy tortilla
crisps, *66*
Chile prawn and mango
cups, *105*
Chile prawn and noodle
salad, *14*
Chocolate and ice cream fillo
sandwiches, *94*
Chocolate dip, Fruit with
creamy, *94*
ciabatta, Mediterranean, *101*
Citrus chicken with garbanzo
salad, *60*
Coffee and raspberry tortes, *97*
Coleslaw with fat-free
dressing, *83*

Corn bread with roast beef,
arugula and horseradish,
100
corn tortilla chips,
Oven-dried, *100*
couscous, Spiced currant, *75*
Crisp green vegetables with
tempeh, *31*
crisps, Potato, *84*
Crunchy baked rosti, *84*
Crusted lamb roast, *46*
Curry
Prawn curry, *33*
Spinach and pumpkin
curry, *32*
Thai-style chicken and
vegetable curry, *32*

Easy niçoise-style salad, *14*
Eggplant, spinach and butter
lettuce salad, *79*
Eggplant, tomato and leek
lasagna, *59*
Eggs with asparagus, grilled
ham and onion jam, *106*

Feta, olive and arugula salad
with roasted tomatoes, *86*
Fish
fillets, Lemony, with
poached leeks, *35*
Pan-fried, with white wine
sauce, *37*
steaks, Grilled, with tangy
salsa, *36*
French fruit toast with maple
yogurt, *110*
French meringues with
berries, *90*
Fresh fruit with passionfruit
yogurt, *93*
Fried rice with prawns, *11*
Fruit cup crush, *109*
Fruit with creamy
chocolate dip, *94*

Garbanzos with sweet potato
and tomato, *30*
Garlic potatoes, *77*
Gazpacho juice, *106*
Ginger, chicken and lime
patties, *41*
Gingered prawn and palm
sugar rolls, *56*
Gnocchi with caramelized
pumpkin and sage sauce, *58*
Green pea puree, *81*

green vegetables, Crisp, with tempeh, *31*
Grilled asparagus, prosciutto and peach salad, *19*
Grilled fish steaks with tangy salsa, *36*
Grilled Asian pear with rosewater syrup, *92*

Ham, avocado and roasted tomato toast, *110*
Herb and garlic toasts, *101*
Herbed chicken kebabs with toasted pecans, *60*
Hoisin pork kebabs with pancakes, *52*
Hummus, *98*

Lamb
Black and white sesame crusted lamb, *43*
Crusted lamb roast, *46*
Lamb and feta rissoles, *43*
Lamb cracker bread with crunchy chile glaze, *20*
Lamb focaccia, *100*
Minted lamb and vermicelli soup, *8*
Tandoori lamb naan, *12*
leek, Brandied carrots and, *79*
Lemony fish fillets with poached leeks, *35*
lentil, Red, salad, *79*
Light 'n' spicy crumbed chicken, *43*
Lime and lemon grass mangoes, *92*
lime, Sparkling, granita, *95*
Long bean and asparagus salad with citrus dressing, *83*
Low-fat Caesar-style salad, *81*
Low-fat toasted muesli, *111*

Mango buttermilk booster, *109*
Mediterranean ciabatta, *101*
Mediterranean-style bell pepper rolls, *30*
meringues, French, with berries, *90*
Minted lamb and vermicelli soup, *8*
Mixed fruit and yogurt drink, *109*
Mixed tomato and pumpkin seed salad, *72*
Mixed vegetables with honey glaze, *85*
Moroccan beef salad with couscous, *6*
muesli, Low-fat toasted, *111*
Mushroom, eggplant and zucchini pizza, *22*

Mushroom salad, Two, *77*
Mushroom, spinach and lemon risotto, *12*

Niçoise-style salad, Easy, *14*

Orange hazelnut beans, *72*
Orange pork medallions with roast vegetables, *62*
Oven-dried tortilla chips, *100*

Pancakes with spiced bananas, *108*
Pan-fried fish with white wine sauce, *37*
Pan-fried turkey with garlic and thyme, *38*
passion fruit yogurt, Fresh fruit with, *93*
Pasta
Chicken, lentil and spinach pasta, *48*
Eggplant, tomato and leek lasagna, *59*
Pasta with feta and red bell pepper dressing, *51*
Pasta with roasted mushrooms and tomato, *49*
Pasta with tomatoes, artichokes and olives, *48*
Pasta with veal and baby beans, *45*
Warm pasta salad with mustard mayonnaise, *16*
Pea and ham soup with sourdough croutons, *54*
Peanut pork steaks, *45*
Petite pecan pies, *97*
pizza, Mushroom, eggplant and zucchini, *22*
Poached chicken with tropical salsa, *40*
Polenta triangles with smoked salmon, *102*
Polenta with tomato, asparagus and watercress, *58*
Pork
Hoisin pork kebabs with pancakes, *52*
Orange pork medallions with roast vegetables, *62*
Peanut pork steaks, *45*
Pork loin with water chestnut and mushroom filling, *62*
Pork, pine nut and Cointreau risotto, *11*
Pork with tomato relish, *44*
Satay pork and noodle stir-fry, *28*
Porridge with sticky fruits, *108*

Potato
Bacon, buttermilk and chive puree, *88*
Crunchy baked rosti, *84*
Garlic potatoes, *77*
Potato cakes, *84*
Potato crisps, *84*
Potato lentil patties, *54*
Potato wedges with two sauces, *102*
Smoky potato salad, *81*
Sourdough, ham and potato bake, *63*
Tomato and basil potatoes, *88*
prawn, Gingered, and palm sugar rolls, *56*
Prawn curry, *33*
Pumpkin and parsnip bake, *86*

Quick banana bread, *111*
Quick beet dip, *98*

Raspberries and watermelon with hazelnut syrup, *93*
Red lentil salad, *79*
Rice
Fried rice with prawns, *11*
Mushroom, spinach and lemon risotto, *12*
Pork, pine nut and Cointreau risotto, *11*
Risotto cakes with basil sauce and pancetta, *56*
Spicy chicken fried rice, *13*
Wild rice salad, *88*
ricotta, Baked lemon-thyme, with sourdough, *102*
Risotto cakes with basil sauce and pancetta, *56*
Roasted baby vegetables in maple syrup, *74*
Roasted bell pepper and olive salad, *76*
Roasted red bell pepper tarts, *67*
Roasted squash and cumin dip, *98*
Rock lobster and raspberry salad, *21*
rosti, Crunchy baked, *85*

Salads
Caesar-style salad, Low-fat, *81*
Chile prawn and noodle salad, *14*
Citrus chicken with garbanzo salad, *60*
Coleslaw with fat-free dressing, *83*
Eggplant, spinach and butter lettuce salad, *79*

Feta, olive and arugula salad with roasted tomatoes, *86*
Grilled asparagus, prosciutto and peach salad, *19*
Long bean and asparagus salad with citrus dressing, *83*
Moroccan beef salad with couscous, *6*
niçoise-style salad, Easy, *14*
Red lentil salad, *79*
Roasted bell pepper and olive salad, *76*
Rock lobster and raspberry salad, *21*
Salmon and dill tortellini salad, *21*
Scallop and goat cheese salad, *17*
Sesame chicken noodle salad, *17*
Smoky potato salad, *81*
Thai beef salad, *68*
tomato and pumpkin seed salad, Mixed, *72*
Tuna bean salad, *19*
Two-mushroom salad, *77*
Warm pasta salad with mustard mayonnaise, *16*
Wild rice salad, *88*
Salmon and dill tortellini salad, *21*
Salmon with dill and caper dressing, *37*
samosas, Bread, *104*
Satay pork and noodle stir-fry, *28*
Scallop and goat cheese salad, *17*
Seafood and Fish
Char-grilled octopus with tomatoes and garbanzos, *65*
Chile prawn and noodle salad, *14*
Fried rice with prawns, *11*
Gingered prawn and palm sugar rolls, *56*
Grilled fish cutlets with tangy salsa, *36*
Lemony fish fillets with poached leeks, *35*
Pan-fried fish with white wine sauce, *37*
Prawn curry, *33*
Rock lobster and raspberry salad, *21*
Salmon and dill tortellini salad, *21*
Salmon with dill and caper dressing, *37*

Scallop and goat cheese salad, 17
Smoked salmon and roasted vegetable cracker bread, 23
Stir-fried prawns and noodles, 28
Tuna bean salad, 19
Tuna with char-grilled vegetables, 35
Seasoned beef tenderloin, 71
Sesame chicken noodle salad, 17
Smoked salmon and r oasted vegetable cracker bread, 23
Smoky potato salad, 81

Soups
Carrot and lentil soup with caraway toast, 55
Chicken, corn and noodle chowder, 8
Minted lamb and vermicelli soup, 8
Pea and ham soup with sourdough croutons, 54
Tomato and cranberry bean soup, 9
Sourdough, ham and potato bake, 63
Sparkling lime granita, 95
Spiced currant couscous, 75
Spicy chicken fried rice, 13
Spicy tomato dip, 101
Spinach and feta focaccia, 100
Spinach and pumpkin curry, 32
squash, Roasted, and cumin dip, 98
Steaks with bell pepper salsa, 46

Stir-fries
Chicken chile stir-fry, 28
Satay pork and noodle stir-fry, 28
Stir-fried Asian greens, 76
Stir-fried Mexican beef, 25
Stir-fried prawns and noodles, 28
Stir-fried turkey with lemon and chile, 27
Sweet soy chicken and noodles, 27
Tofu and spinach stir-fry, 71
Sweet potato and corn frittata, 66

Sweet soy chicken and noodles, 27
Swiss muesli with grilled mangoes and blueberries, 106

Tandoori chicken bites, 104
Tandoori lamb naan, 12
Teriyaki beef skewers, 65
Thai beef salad, 68
Thai-style chicken and vegetable curry, 32
Tofu and spinach stir-fry, 71
Tomato and basil potatoes, 88
Tomato and cranberry bean soup, 9
tomato and pumpkin seed salad, Mixed, 72
tomato, Spicy, dip, 101
Tuna bean salad, 19
Tuna with char-grilled vegetables, 35
turkey, Pan-fried, with garlic and thyme, 38
turkey, Stir-fried, with lemon and chile, 27
Two-mushroom salad, 77

Vanilla ricotta mousse, 90
Veal rib chops with warm tomato-caper salsa, 68
veal and baby beans, Pasta with, 45
Vegetable rolls with dipping sauce, 105

Vegetables
Bacon, buttermilk and chive puree, 88
Beans and sugar snap peas with lemon and capers, 74
Brandied carrots and leek, 79
Crunchy baked rosti, 84
Green pea puree, 81
Mixed vegetables with honey glaze, 85
Orange hazelnut beans, 72
Potato cakes, 84
Potato crisps, 84
Pumpkin and parsnip bake, 86
Roasted baby vegetables in maple syrup, 74
Stir-fried Asian greens, 76
Tomato and basil potatoes, 88

White beans in rich tomato sauce, 86
Zucchini, squash and fava bean medley, 82

Vegetarian
Carrot and lentil soup with caraway toast, 55
Chile beans with spicy tortilla crisps, 66
Crisp green vegetables with tempeh, 31
Eggplant, tomato and leek lasagna, 59
Garbanzos with sweet potato and tomato, 30
Gnocchi with caramelized pumpkin and sage sauce, 58
Mediterranean-style bell pepper rolls, 30
Mushroom, eggplant and zucchini pizza, 22
Mushroom, spinach and lemon risotto, 12
Pasta with feta and red bell pepper dressing, 51
Pasta with roasted mushrooms and tomato, 49
Pasta with tomatoes, artichokes and olives, 48
Polenta with tomato, asparagus and watercress, 58
Potato lentil patties, 54
Roasted red bell pepper tarts, 67
Spinach and pumpkin curry, 32
Sweet potato and corn frittata, 66
Tofu and spinach stir-fry, 71
Tomato and cranberry bean soup, 9

Warm pasta salad with mustard mayonnaise, 16
Watermelon mint ice, 95
White beans in rich tomato sauce, 86
Wild rice salad, 88

Zucchini, squash and fava bean medley, 82

MAKE YOUR OWN STOCK

These recipes can be made up to 4 days ahead and stored, covered, in the refrigerator. Be sure to remove any fat from the surface after the cooled stock has been refrigerated overnight. If the stock is to be kept longer, it is best to freeze it in smaller quantities.

Stock is also available in cans or aseptic packs. Bouillon cubes or granules can be used. As a guide, 1 teaspoon of bouillon granules or 1 small crumbled bouillon cube mixed with 1 cup water will give a fairly strong stock. Be aware of the salt and fat content of bouillon cubes and granules and prepared stocks.

All stock recipes make about 10 cups.

BEEF STOCK
4 lb meaty beef bones
2 medium onions
2 stalks celery, chopped
2 medium carrots, chopped
3 bay leaves
2 teaspoons black peppercorns
20 cups water
12 cups water, extra

Place bones and unpeeled chopped onions in baking dish. Bake in 450°F oven about 1 hour or until bones and onions are well browned. Transfer bones and onions to large pan, add celery, carrots, bay leaves, peppercorns and water, simmer, uncovered, 3 hours. Add extra water, simmer, uncovered, further 1 hour; strain.

CHICKEN STOCK
4 lb chicken bones
2 medium onions, chopped
2 stalks celery, chopped
2 medium carrots, chopped
3 bay leaves
2 teaspoons black peppercorns
20 cups water

Combine all ingredients in large pan, simmer, uncovered, 2 hours; strain.

FISH STOCK
3 lb fish bones
12 cups water
1 medium onion, chopped
2 stalks celery, chopped
2 bay leaves
1 teaspoon black peppercorns

Combine all ingredients in large pan, simmer, uncovered, 20 minutes; strain.

VEGETABLE STOCK
2 large carrots, chopped
2 large parsnips, chopped
4 medium onions, chopped
12 stalks celery, chopped
4 bay leaves
2 teaspoons black peppercorns
24 cups water

Combine all ingredients in large pan, simmer, uncovered, 1 1/2 hours; strain.

Add these new Cole's Home Library mini menu cookbooks to your collection

mini books
maxi results

fit for life – **healthy eating**

make it tonight – good food fast

COOKERY

The Essential Barbecue Cookbook

Enjoying the best the barbecue has to offer, this innovative collection of recipes is all you need to prepare fabulous dishes and outdoor meals. *The Essential Barbecue Cookbook* covers cooking beef, veal, poultry, lamb, seafood, pork and vegetables, along with taste-tempting breads and desserts. All your questions are answered about gas and charcoal cooking fuel sources, grill gadgets and we show you how to buy and look after your grill. Barbecuing is no longer a summer-time-only pursuit. So, anytime of the year, fire up the barbecue and impress family and friends with these easy-to-prepare recipes for all open kettle and gas grills. Over 180 recipes, including full glossary and index.
ISBN 1-56426-153-0 $11.95

Meals-in-Minutes

Fast, simple and healthy are the catch cries for today's busy lifestyle. *Meals-in-Minutes* is specially designed for the enthusiastic cook with little time. This exciting collection proves that fast food can also be good food – good for you, good to eat, good and tasty. Some of the recipes featured take just a few minutes while others can be prepared ahead of time for quick dining after work or when family meals are needed in a hurry. All recipes use simple ingredients for exciting results and have all been triple tested for flavor and easy preparation. *Meals-in Minutes* will become a kitchen standby. Over 180 recipes, including full glossary and index.
ISBN 1-56426-150-6-0 $11.95

Oodles of Noodles

Noodles are the new pasta! Versatile and delicious, there's an almost limitless variety of noodles available: fresh or dried, rice, wheat or flour, egg or eggless. With this Home Library original, you'll learn to use your noodles and your culinary success will be assured. This special collection covers soups, starters and finger food, salads, stir-fries and main meals all featuring fabulous noodles in all their guises. Meat dishes, chicken and other poultry, seafood and vegetarian delights are all included. Samples of each noodle, before and after cooking, make this collection particularly easy to use and we also include shopping and noodle preparation tips. Over 120 traditional and innovative recipes, including full glossary and index.
ISBN 1-56426-151-4 $11.95

Not-So-Humble Vegetables

This A-Z stroll through the vegie patch is both a visual and culinary treat. Starting at A for Artichoke through to Z for Zucchini, this special collection will tempt all the senses. Menu planning becomes very easy and exciting with this huge array of main dishes, accompaniments and side dishes. With new varieties readily available in most supermarkets and green grocers, enjoying the world of vegetables is becoming a favorite pastime of city dwellers and suburbanites alike. No longer second-best to meat and seafood, vegetables now step into the spotlight and their infinite variety of tastes, textures and colours is dazzling. Over 180 recipes, including glossary, nutrition guide and index.
ISBN 1-56426-152-2 $11.95

Creative Cooking on a Budget

Cooking on a budget can have a fun and creative side. The challenge of feeding family and friends delicious and exciting meals without spending a fortune brings out the inventor as well as the chef in the most hesitant of cooks. These triple-tested healthy and achievable recipes are as affordable as they are delectable. They use readily available ingredients to make exciting and inexpensive meals, and you will be inspired to dream up your own creations. These fabulous recipes will also convince you that home cooking is not only infinitely better but far more inexpensive than over-priced take-out foods. Over 130 recipes, with hints on how to keep cooking costs low with no sacrifice of taste, full glossary and index.
ISBN 1-56426-157-3 $11.95